God & the Modern World

God & the Modern World

Julia Watkin

Marquette University Press
2005

MARQUETTE
UNIVERSITY

PRESS

Library of Congress Cataloging-in-Publication Data

Watkin, Julia.
    God & the modern world / Julia Watkin.
        p. cm. — (Marquette studies in philosophy ; no. 41)
    Includes bibliographical references and index.
    ISBN-13: 978-0-87462-664-3 (pbk. : alk. paper)
    ISBN-10: 0-87462-664-1 (pbk. : alk. paper)
    1. God. 2. Religion and science. I. Title: God and the modern world. II. Title.
III. Series.
    BT103.W38 2005
    231—dc22
                                        2005006134

**Photo of Le Corbusier's Notre Dame du Haut
at Ronchamp, France, by Andrew J. Tallon**

Association of American
University Presses

MARQUETTE UNIVERSITY PRESS
MILWAUKEE

The Association of Jesuit University Presses

Table of Contents

Dedication 7

Acknowledgements 8

Introduction 9

Chapter One: God and Supernature 11
(a) The Grosbøll Affair 11
(b) Clearing the Ground 13
(c) Two Modern Misconceptions 15
(d) God as a Metaphysical Concept 21
(e) Descriptions and Pictures of God 30

Chapter Two: Communication of the Divine—Communication with the Divine 35
(a) Indicators of an Actual Divine Transcendence 35
(b) Some Conceptual Difficulties Concerning Descriptions of the Self 39
(c) On Manifestations of an Actually Transcendent Divinity 43
(d) Forms in which Divinity Manifests Itself 46
(e) Something about Prayer 50

Chapter Three: About Miracles 61
(a) The Definition of a Miracle 61
(b) Hume's Essay "On Miracles 64
(c) Hume and the Violated Laws of Nature 66
(d) Miracles and Modern Objections 69
(e) Epilogue - On the Status of the Divine Miracle-Worker 74

Chapter Four: The Darwinian Red Herring 79
(a) Creation Accounts in the Book of Genesis 79

(b) Darwin's Theory of Evolution 84
(c) Modern Evolution Theory 89
(d) Concepts of Evolution 94
(e) An Unintended Red Herring.. 99
Conclusion.. 102

Notes 107

Bibliography.. 113

Index 125

tilegnet

Søren Kierkegaard

Acknowledgements

Grateful thanks to Richard Milton, who kindly read and commented on the Darwin section in this book, and to Gordon Marino, Linn Miller, John and Barbara Norris, Bob and Sylvia Perkins, for being so supportive concerning this project. Also my thanks to the wonderful library staff at the University of Tasmania, and to Andy Tallon at Marquette University Press for all his help in getting the book ready for publication.

God and the Modern World
Introduction

Besides buildings and monuments from an earlier time, a walk in Vor Frue Plads, the cathedral square of the city of Copenhagen, presents to the careful observer an interesting contrast between religion and science. Outside the old university building can be seen a bust of physicist Niels Bohr (1885-1962), famous for his work in atomic physics and not least for his use of the idea of "complementarity" to deal with the fact that matter and radiation can be viewed as waves and particles. Under his bust is carved the Yin Yang symbol from Taoism, which Bohr used to indicate what he saw as the union of the two conflicting positions. If one walks further along the square one comes to the Bishop's palace. Above the palace doorway is an inscription from the Bible: Philippians 3 v 20: "Thi vort Borgerskab er i himlene"—"We...are citizens of heaven" (Bible 1989). The writer of the letter to the Philippians, Paul of Tarsus, wrote as a committed Christian, and thus as one concerned with issues in the field of religion. For many, for example astronomer Jens Martin Knudsen (Knudsen 2003), the two men can be seen as concerned with totally different areas of life that contribute to our entire understanding of existence. Yet there are others for whom the world of science presents a challenge to the world of religion, not least to Christianity and theism. For these, Paul is seen merely as writing in the context of an outdated understanding of creation, whereas Bohr and fellow scientists are viewed as unlocking the basic secrets of the universe.

There has been an enormous debate about the relation between religion and science, with a huge and continuing literature on the subject. While some scientists, e.g. physical chemist Peter Atkins and biologist Richard Dawkins (Atkins 1994; Dawkins 1991), think science excludes the possibility of God's existence, others, such as physicists John Polkinghorne and Russell Stannard (Polkinghorne 1998; Stannard 1993), take the opposite view. On what one might call the religious front, the 20th and 21st centuries have produced the phenomenon of pastors either denying the existence of God or seeking to present a radical interpretation of the concept of God that excludes any notion of a supernatural transcendence. This, of course, is not something that has happened out of the blue (Kent 1982; Macquarrie 1971), and the pastors do not stand alone in having problems with traditional ideas about God and other related topics in the field of religion. Members of the laity also grapple with these issues. For example, in Christianity, subjects such as creation and divine intervention are related bones of contention.

In this book I would like to share with you my thoughts about some of these thorny issues, not least because I am convinced that in some circles of debate there is serious confusion concerning discussion about God, a confusion that needs its opposite, namely an attempt at clarification. Because of space limitations and the need to avoid complexity, I will omit many qualifications and depth of detail in order that the main outline of what I wish to say can stand out clearly. I will be concentrating particularly on the Christian tradition, because this has been the background of my own life as a western European, and it also provides good examples of issues that I want to address.

Julia Watkin
Copenhagen, Denmark
and Launceston, Tasmania 2003-2004

Chapter One
God and Supernature

In this chapter I will first present material concerning the debate surrounding a Danish pastor who publicly asserted his views about God. I have selected the case of Thorkild Grosbøll because his is an excellent example of a fundamental confusion concerning thought about God. I will then go on to discuss what I see to be the two main elements of the confusion, with discussion of the views of the Sea of Faith group and former bishop Spong. I will argue that such views are clouded by two basic misconceptions, and that the notion of "the death of God" has more to do with issues in philosophy and science than with the arena of theology. Finally I will discuss the status of descriptions or pictures of God.

(a) The Grosbøll Affair

In 2003, pastor Thorkild Grosbøll caused a stir in Denmark when he published a book which, he stated at the outset, did not have anything about "any creating and sustaining God, no conception of a resurrection or an eternal life" because that kind of thing had never said anything to him, not even when he was a child (Grosbøll 2003b, 9). This, combined with an interview drawing attention to the book and other statements in it (Grosbøll 2003c),[1] provoked an enormous debate in the Danish press, both about his permitted continuance as a pastor in the national church and not least about whether his thinking was acceptable from a theological standpoint. Theology professor Theodor Jørgensen said that Grosbøll confidently rejected fixed ideas about who God was, but then immediately fixed fast the concept of God according to his own ideas (Jørgensen 2003, 4). Jørgensen suggested that Grosbøll's theology could be seen as a continuation of the "God is dead" theology of the 1950s, though of course this phrase is already famous as a Nietzsche theme (Altizer &

Hamilton 1968; Nietzsche 1974, 181-82). Grosbøll himself, who for a time was suspended from his pastorate,[2] said in a newspaper article (Grosbøll 2003d) that he regretted the public effect of his statements, but rejected what he saw as an antiquated world-view and language about God. In this article he also defined God as meaning that: "a person is to be a person—without secret access to the supernatural. Such a life corresponds to God existing." In a report of a lecture given by Grosbøll (Korsholm 2003), he was asked at the lecture whether he believed in God, yes or no. His reply was to refer the questioner to his book. When pressed by others on this issue, he said he believed in God if he could avoid people getting a picture of God in their heads from the Middle Ages. In an earlier press article (Høgsbro 2003) Bente Høgsbro complained about the use by Grosbøll, and those sharing his views, of the "Middle Ages" label for those who believed in God, and asked what assertions made by the theologically educated about bringing the Christian faith up-to-date meant.

Not surprisingly, many felt confused by the apparent contradiction implicit in Grosbøll's statements that he didn't believe in God and then that he did believe. For his part, Grosbøll was annoyed that people didn't seem to understand him, yet he himself did not appear to understand the puzzlement of those who saw their religious beliefs rejected as a product of the Middle Ages and were wanting to know exactly what was to be updated with Christianity. Throughout the entire debate, many seemed not to notice that two major questions had become tangled together, so that in the press discussion, answers were frequently given to one question that had in fact to do with the other. This was especially evident in the lecture report and also to an extent in Grosbøll's post suspension article (Grøsboll 2003d). In a postscript to their book, Svend Bjerg and Palle Steffensen also draw attention to the confusion of the two questions (Bjerg & Steffensen 2003, 162-66 esp. 165).

The first question has to do with whether or not there is a God or conscious divine agency not dependent on humans, and in connection with this, whether there is an eternal life, or life after an individual's death. The second question has to do with which descriptions or pictures of God are factually or morally acceptable. This is not to say that the two questions can somehow be kept totally independent of each other, but it is important to keep them separate during debate if one is to avoid the kind of confusion occurring in the Grosbøll affair. It is my contention that this confusion has plagued much general debate about issues having to do with God.

(b) Clearing the Ground

Our first question, then, has to do with whether there is a God in some way above or beyond our daily world. In speaking of this possibility, I will use the term "actual transcendence" or "actually transcendent" to make clear that I am not thinking of transcendence understood only as something higher than material human affairs, for example, moral or other values by which a person lives. In connection with the existence of such a transcendent God, I also include the notion of the reality of another sphere of existence, a sphere that has been referred to, e.g., as "heaven," "eternity," "eternal life," or "life after death." When speaking about this sphere of existence I will use the term "transcendent sphere of existence" to make clear that I am not thinking of the use of the term "eternal life" to describe only some purely human quality of existence, for example, living as a loving person open to the needs of others.

Philosopher Bernard Williams uses, as a test of whether a person is believing in Christianity or not, the criterion that God is transcendent to humans and human affairs, meaning that God would exist even if there were no human beings. He thinks that if this criterion is not met, then one has to do with some form of religious humanism (Williams 1968, 53). This criterion could be applied within the context of a number of religions asserting the existence of a transcendent God, and so we here should not think exclusively of Christianity where the existence of God is concerned. What is important, however, is that there are those aiming to stay within the Christian tradition, or at least within the tradition of religious belief, who would reject Williams' criterion. A good example of this is Anglican pastor and academic Don Cupitt and members of the "Sea of Faith"[3] group he inspired. For the Sea of Faith group there is no God outside human consciousness. God is not in any way a supernatural being; God-talk is a way of referring to important values. The notion of transcendence can thus refer only to values that a person sets above him or herself as moral guidelines, or else it is the encounter with the future and experiences over which one has no control. So when one dies, one's conscious life is ended. There is no life after death. While the Sea of Faith group seems to be particularly directed against religious fundamentalism, it views all those who believe there is a God outside human consciousness, and who do think there is a life after death, as being in error. It would therefore like the various churches to "come to terms with modernity" (ABC Australia 2003).

Here we can recognize the position of pastor Grosbøll, and we can note something else, namely, that whereas opponents of Grosbøll and the Sea of Faith group have concentrated on religious assumptions about God, by contrast little has been said about what seems to me to be a basic issue, namely, how those sharing the outlook of Grosbøll and members of the Sea of Faith group view science. I will come back to this when I have looked at a position that seems to me to stand between those who believe in an actual transcendence and those who do not. The position I have in mind is well represented by former bishop Spong, who, like Grosbøll and members of the Sea of Faith group, has problems with traditional statements made about God and argues that Christianity must change or it will die. For Spong, God is "the ultimate reality" in his life, a "universal presence undergirding all of life," and he says he lives in a constant awareness of the divine presence. He also affirms his belief in an eternal life not only now, but forever. He sees religion as a human attempt to "process the God experience," but his main God descriptor is "the Ground of Being," a term he inherits from his teacher Paul Tillich. Spong thus rejects "theism," understanding this to indicate belief in a rather literal heaven and in an external supernatural God who knows and is in control of everything (Spong 1999, 3, 140, 226, 210, 218, 228, 225, 224, 204-05, 41, 130, 6-11; Tillich 1962). Yet Spong at the same time asserts belief in God and a transcendent sphere of existence, and while rejecting the statements of traditional Christian theism, retains an actual transcendence in a different form. God's reality is not identical with human life, but at the same time Spong does not want to indicate a separation between the two. God is not to be seen as a personal being, but as a presence within the fabric of life, manifested in "the personal being of the whole creation" (Spong 1999, 68, 130,

177, 193, 196, 201). Spong thus wants to liberate his religious belief from any notion of God as above or beyond the universe, a personal being in charge of things, yet while he speaks of "the Being of God" and "the Ground of Being," and God as "present in all of life," he still uses terms such as "transcendent," "transcendence," and "eternal life." For Spong, God is not only the Ground of Being, but is also "over, under, around, and through the very fabric of life" (Spong 1999, 193, 218, 210, 217, 130, 196). To sum up here, Spong in places somewhat confusingly continues to use a reinterpreted terminology of transcendence, and he does so in the light of his acceptance of the death of the personal, transcendent God of theism (Spong 1999, 60, 70, 98, 132, 176-77, 140-41, 160, 182-83, 219, 226). Yet in relation to Bernard Williams' criterion, we can say that Spong's view seems to meet it, as long as there is life, and particularly conscious life, in the universe. It is not clear, however, despite his references to eternal and timeless life, whether, or in what way, Spong's God would exist if there were no human beings and our universe had come to its final end, so that there was no life anywhere.

(c) Two Modern Misconceptions

Common to the Sea of Faith people, Grosbøll, Spong and many others, however, is the idea that we need to face up to "premodern misunderstandings." We live in a "postmodern" world; we need to be "progressive" and accept "modernity." (Spong 1999, 140, 226; ABC Australia 2003). In other words, Christianity, and other religions laying claim to an actually transcendent God, are out of date in their ideas; they need to bring them in line with all that we know in our time, especially in the field of the sciences. I will here argue that there are two major problems with such statements. The first is what I will call the myth of progress (see Dawson 1945). It is tacitly assumed that whatever is new in the realm of ideas and discoveries must be better and more accurate than what has gone before, and we are getting more and more accurate all the time. So anything seen as incompatible with the modern world must be outlawed as erroneous. While this is true of a great number of things, and we have made enormous advances in many areas, especially the sciences, we need to free ourselves from the naïve idea that we live in a scientific world that is gradually completing an inevitably accurate picture of the entire universe in all its details. Lord Kelvin (1824-1907), resting secure in 19th century classical physics, thought then that physics was nearing completion as a subject and that he could be definite as to the age of the earth and sun. Yet the Newtonian universe gave way to Einstein's picture of existence, and it was realized that one could not rest in any certainty that the current scientific picture of the universe would not undergo further marked changes. In 1962, Thomas Kuhn presented his theory of paradigms to explain shifts in the history of science as the history of the career of changing paradigms or scientific unitary pictures of how things are (Appleyard 1992, 116; Kuhn 1996). Although in the light of criticism Kuhn modified his position in the second edition of his book, paying more attention to the control of theory by experiment, and to the possibility of criteria not tied to particular paradigms, his view made a big impact on how science is seen.

Despite this, the optimism continued in certain circles that science would soon complete the big picture of things. In 1980, Stephen Hawking thought that the end was in sight for theoretical physics, with the production of "a complete, consistent, and unified theory of the physical interactions that would describe all possible observations." This theory has been popularly labelled "the theory of everything" (Hawking 1993b, 49-68; Hawking 1988, esp. 165-66). Naturally neither Hawking, nor those sharing his optimism, thought that such a theory could be arrived at without scientific trial and error on the way. One has only to remember the acceptance, between 1864 and 1887, of the existence of the mysterious medium known as "ether," as an example of scientific acceptance of something later rejected (Appleyard 1992, 145-46; Pais 1991, 66-68). It can be noted that where there is resistance to new ideas with implied or manifest implications for the entire picture of things—we can here think of Lord Kelvin's initial rejection of X-rays as a hoax, or John Taylor's rejection of the idea of radiation from black holes (Kuhn 1996, 59; Hawking 1988, 112)—the resistance is directed to the future. A person who thinks the current scientific world picture is correct, minus a few details, is not ready to concede the possibility of some radical change occurring in that picture, even though that person comes later to accept the change or changes.

There is, however, the rejection of ideas where the resistance is directed towards the past. A classic example of this is theologian Rudolf Bultmann (1884-1976), who stated that: "It is impossible to use electric light and the wireless and to avail ourselves of modern medical and surgical discoveries, and at the same time to believe in the New Testament world of spirits and miracles" (Bultmann 1961, 1-44 esp. 5). Bultmann, when he wrote this in 1941, did so in a pre-Kuhnian context, assuming a closed world of causes and effects in the field of science. Yet Bultmann was, and is, not alone in rejecting past ideas that do not fit in with the state of modern knowledge. Considering what we do now know in the modern world, such an attitude is, of course, justified concerning many things. We know, for example, that demons are not the cause of epilepsy; we know the earth is a spherical minor planet in a galaxy, and so on. There are countless things that we definitely do now know that our ancestors did not.

Yet just as caution may be initially needed with respect to apparent new discoveries in relation to our current state of knowledge, and despite the very many things we do know, caution is also needed in relation to the past. Bultmann could well reject the New Testament notion of spirits or demons causing sickness, but, as I will show later, his rejection of miracles cannot be so easily accepted. Similarly, it is obvious that we do not live in a physical 3-tiered universe with a physical hell and heaven above the earth, but it is somewhat premature to reject the idea of a supernature or to reject entirely the notion of theism, and of God's externality to the universe (Spong 1999, 16, 40-41, 138, 181-83, 204-05, 208-09, 220, 140, 176, 178, 226). Recalling, however, that for Grosbøll and the Sea of Faith group there is no God or conscious divine agency not dependent on humans, no eternal life, or life after the individual's death, their rejection clearly concerns the first question about God, though in the case of Grosbøll, in sermons published in 1988 (Grosbøll 2003a, 29-31), he seems at that point to suggest somewhat agnostically a vague belief in something or other that set the universe going "beyond time and space, beyond infinity," though at the same time he puts forward the possibility that perhaps God is the universe and we are his thoughts, or that God may even be the dynamic movement of the big bang. Spong, on the other hand, replaces an actually transcendent God with the idea of

God as totally immanent,[4] and his rejection can be seen to be one of rejecting particular descriptions and pictures of God. Yet for Spong, Grosbøll, and the Sea of Faith group, the notion of a personal deity seems equally dead (Spong 1999, 183; Grosbøll 2003a, 29; Grosbøll 2003b, 9; ABC Australia 2003). It is here, however, that we arrive at a second modern misunderstanding concerning talk about God, namely the myth of universal beliefs.

In the writings of those rejecting an actually transcendent God and particular descriptions of that God, it is not uncommon to encounter the notion that when certain people believe certain things, they must all have the same conception of what they believe. In connection with this is the tendency to lump large groups of people together in single categories of believers or non-believers in specific things. To take the second part of the myth of universal beliefs first, one can note the tendency to use the plural concerning belief, or words indicating that many or most belong to the particular belief group in question. For example, pastor Grosbøll confidently asserts that "the words of the creed represent all that we can't bring ourselves to say....We don't believe in God...." He also speaks of "our picture of the world," as if there is one uniform view of the world in modern times (Grosbøll 2003b, 147-48, 39). The Sea of Faith group (ABC Australia 2003), less assertively, and more cautiously, tells us that "people are horrified to discover that religious beliefs...have melted away from them" and that members of the group are "in the minority" among believers. "Many more people are turning to fundamentalist beliefs." While it is true that some are turning to fundamentalism and others have lost faith in religious beliefs, the use of "people" and "many" in the context of the documentary about the group still rather suggests numbers of people losing a particular set of religious beliefs and opting to join the Sea of Faith minority, when they are not opting for religious fundamentalism. Spong also tends to talk in terms of groups with his reference to "a countless host of modern men and women" who have problems with traditional religious views, the "silent majority of believers..." (Spong 1999, 4). Nor is Bultmann free from a touch of universal pluralism when he implies that there is a general impossibility of belief where miracles are concerned (Bultmann 1961, 5).

We can also note here that where people are lumped together in categories in this manner, the categories are often limited, and other in between categories are ignored. For example, not all religious groups are fundamentalist, yet when the Sea of Faith group criticizes religious fundamentalism, one rather gets the impression from the Compass documentary that those not busily being modern in their ideas must be naughty reactionary fundamentalists retreating from modern life. I emphasize that I am not disputing that people change concerning what they believe, nor am I denying that they can be troubled by aspects of traditional religious beliefs. It is the tendency to lump people together in categories that is unfortunate.

This brings me to the first part of the myth of universal beliefs, where the same conceptual belief content is ascribed to people in the various groups. This does not, of course, mean that no one shares the same ideas, but it is surely naive to lump people together uniformly under one particular label. This tendency to think individuals share exactly the same concepts is strange when pluralism is recognized where groups are concerned. The fact of major religions besides Christianity, and of various new age religions, can be made part of the argument for the need to modernize Christian concepts, yet that individuals in the various groups do not necessarily believe the same things seems to be ignored by the modernizers. If we take the label "fundamentalist" as an example, and here stay with Christianity, it is clear that groups of fundamentalists, and even individuals in the particular groups, do not necessarily believe exactly the same things. As an example of what I mean, I can mention an incident in the 1970s in Copenhagen, when I was the guest of a fundamentalist Christian at a summer festival. At the festival were members of his group, but also of another Christian fundamentalist group. It was explained to me by the member of the first group that the other group did not believe in the right way, because they held different opinions to the first group on points of doctrine. People in "modern life" in fact believe a variety of things about secular and religious matters. The tendency to lump people together in groups is thus highly dubious, and closely linked to the assumption that individuals in a group all assent to a specific set of uniform concepts or ideas. Here I can cite the case of a lady I once knew who lived at Glastonbury in England. She was a devout Anglican, yet when one began talking to her, it soon emerged that she had a complex set of beliefs mixed in with her Anglicanism, involving a group centred on the Glastonbury Chalice well (see Villiers 1968).

When those who subscribe to forms of the death of God class those who do not with fundamentalists (or with people from the Middle Ages), there are thus two things going on: the theists are lumped together in a group, but they also have ascribed to them a uniform description of how they conceptualize a theistic God. It seems to be presupposed that this group holds specific literal (and erroneous) conceptions about God and the universe. This is why, in her article about pastor Grosbøll and others, Bente Høgsbro resented being put together with people in the Middle Ages just because she believed in God and held particular beliefs about Jesus (Høgsbro 2003). Yet when Grosbøll and Spong and those like them refer to erroneous concepts in the 13th century and earlier, and contrast the faith of people in the past with the faith of people today (Grosbøll 2003b, 16; Spong 1999, 16, 29-34, 116, 202-03), they not only presuppose what individuals today think when they say they believe in an actually transcendent God, they also presuppose that people in the more distant past all believed in a physical 3-tier universe with God as an old man with a white beard. While it is true that people then had certain physical conceptions about the universe, e.g., in Old Testament times that there were waters above the sky,[5] and some may well have thought of heaven in physical-material terms even in the Middle Ages, it is naïve to assume that people then or at any time all believed in a physical 3-tier universe with such a God. If one turns to the 14th century anonymous work, *The Cloud of Unknowing*, one finds that although the author believed in an almighty, personal, God, and in Christian concepts, such as purgatory and the Day of Judgement, he does not subscribe to the idea of God as an old man in a physical heaven. He responds to the question of how one is to think of God by saying he does not know, and that "of God himself can no man think." God can be encountered only by love of God, but not by thought. God adapts his Godhead "to our power to comprehend." The author of the book also warns against taking physically what is meant spiritually. When he speaks of "deep down in the spirit," for example, he warns against taking the words "in" and "up" literally. "God is a spirit," not a material being. The author also makes a clear distinction between love of God and love of people. There is no question of "God" somehow meaning only the activity of loving one's neighbour (*Cloud of Unknowing* 1961 [1978], 60-61, 64, 84, 67-68, 62, 98, 121, 66, 116, 93).

When we look back to the past as well as consider what people think in the present, we are thus faced with a situation of great complexity. There is a wide variety of individual beliefs, and even groups can be seen to contain a wide variety of sub-groups. So just as there is a great complexity concerning the relationship between science and religious belief, such that generalizations should be avoided (Brooke 1991), so also should universalizations and generalizations be avoided not least where the topic of belief in God is concerned.

(d) God as a Metaphysical Concept

Our first question had to do with whether or not there is a God. I pointed out earlier that where death of God thinkers are concerned, their problems about God seemed to have more to do with issues in science, and one can add, also philosophy, than with religious questions. This is because a lot depends on how people view the universe as a whole. Questions about the existence of a God or divine power turn out, in fact, to be metaphysical questions. The word "metaphysics" is used here specifically to mean what lies beyond our natural, physical world, questions that concern the ultimate nature of reality. Questions about God and about the ultimate origin of the universe are thus metaphysical ones. Whereas physics and other sciences can tell us many things about our finite universe, what they cannot do is tell us about ultimate origins. Many attempts have been made to do so. For example, philosopher Gottfried Leibniz (1646-1716) argued that there has to be a "sufficient" explanatory reason for the existence of everything and that God was that ultimate reason. In our time, physical chemist Peter Atkins has argued that the universe emerged by chance out of pre-primordial dust (Leibniz 1973, 136-44 esp. 137; Atkins 1994, 128-43). In both cases, however, we are dealing with presuppositions beyond the reach of the sciences.

Leibniz is unable to escape the possibility that the universe itself may be basically eternal in some way. For example, there may be a permanent super universe that generates finite universes. Also, if one accepts Leibniz's use of God as the explanation of the universe, there is still no explanation why there was a God or anything. Similarly, Atkins does not seem to be able to explain where the pre-primordial dust came from. Or if it was just "there," we still lack the explanation of why it was there. In both cases, the presuppositions of God and chance activity are taken as basic assumptions, and if we accept either, we still have no answer to the question why. So with the two approaches to investigation of the universe, the "what" of the universe, what it is and how it works, and the "why," whenever a scientist or anyone else goes beyond the what/how side of things into "why" questions, he or she has gone into the area of metaphysical assumptions. Even the scope of what/how questions can be limited in some areas, notably in the long effort by scientists to reach back to the very start of the universe (Hawking 1988, 46, 122).

Three views about the origins of the universe are that the universe started through the factor of chance, or that it started because a fundamental law necessitated its being, or that the universe was started by design or by a designer. There are naturally very many views and variations on these three approaches.—I omit here consideration of the anthropic principle, that the universe is the way it is because otherwise we would not be here to observe it, because at best, despite the amazing fine-tuning, it only underlines the fact that the universe developed according to laws and principles that permitted life in it. It can be noted, however, that John Polkinghorne in his discussion of the principle concludes that anthropic considerations may be part of a cumulative case for theism (Polkinghorne 1996a, 80-92; see Barrow & Tipler 1986).

For Peter Atkins, the universe began through chance. Yet as we saw earlier, Stephen Hawking (along with others) thinks that there is a final, simple law, a "theory of everything," and that when scientists eventually arrive at it, we will have a complete understanding of the entire universe (Hawking 1988, 11-12, 69, 168-69, 175, 136).[6] Physicist Paul Davies has concluded that the universe began through the agency of design or a designer. Even though one cannot have certainty in a metaphysical area, he has favoured divine design as the most probable answer, because he thought an alternative multi-universe solution can explain only a limited range of features of the universe, and it does not account for the lawlike nature of our universe (Davies 1992, 220).[7] With each of the three scientists a common factor is that they have reflected about the structure of the universe and its physical origins before opting for their particular metaphysical assumption concerning what started things off. Where those not so well-versed in science are concerned, it needs to be asked whether, and how, they have reflected about such matters.

In the case of pastor Grosbøll, when he says statements about God and an eternal life have never said anything to him (Grosbøll 2003b, 9), he does not give the reason why. There is thus, at least in his book *En sten i skoen* [A Stone in One's Shoe], nothing to tell us what he thought about the universe as a boy or now as a grown man, while his earlier deliberations in his 1988 sermons *På Sporet af Gud* [On the Track of God] seem chiefly to indicate an understanding of God as the dynamic universe somehow bringing itself about (Grosbøll 2003a, 29-31). In his initial statement to the press in *Weekendavisen* (Grosbøll 2003c), he merely asserts he does not believe in God as the explanation for everything, and that "no one in ordinary life operates with the concept of a God-sustained universe. We function on the premises of science." One might guess that Grosbøll, in the face of neo-Darwinistic evolutionary theory and descriptions of the universe starting with a big bang, may for this reason believe any thought of an actually transcendent God or eternal life to be impossible.

Where the emphasis in some descriptions is on the universe viewed as a bundle of particles and objects, one is encouraged to think only of the possible "fate of the atoms of our bodies" when the universe reaches its end. As evolved creatures with, it is presupposed by some, mind or consciousness identified only with the physical brain and its activity, there seems to be no place for more than our short lives in this world (Boslough 1989, 96; see Churchland 1988). Obviously one does not know whether pastor Grosbøll has been influenced by a far too limited contact with what are huge and complex issues in philosophy and science. It may be that he simply finds it impossible to conceptualize possibilities in the area of metaphysics. Some people find it impossible to fit ideas of God or eternal life into what appears to be an everyday material world. Also, if, like former British pastor Michael Goulder, one has never had any experience of a divine presence of any kind, it is only honest to admit failure to believe. Nor can one blame such a pastor if, instead of resigning a pastorate, he or she first tries hard to find other ways of making sense of the concept of God. What is not acceptable, however, is that such a person tries to decide that notions of an actually transcendent God and supernature are to be rejected by everyone else (Cupitt 1982, xii-xiv; Goulder & Hick 1983, esp. 29-30).

The problem lies with the fact that not only is one into the area of metaphysics, but one also in thinking about God is conceptualizing. The author of *The Cloud of Unknowing* was aware of the trap and urges us to avoid it—something that is difficult if one is a philosopher of religion. We are, however, well able to recognize that our conceptualizing is limited by a host of things: by our lack of access to more than a fragment of scholarship in key areas, by the fact that we have to set limits to the areas of our research and discussion, and by the fact that we are not capable of getting into the minds of every individual on the planet and laying out scientifically precisely what they think when they hear the words "God" and "eternal life." There is a variety of ways in which people have considered the idea of God and the universe, but initially it is important how the universe is viewed. For example, one may have a totally materialistic view of the universe as consisting purely of matter or of purely finite energy particles giving the appearance of matter. One may, like the German philosopher G.W.F. Hegel (1770-1831), think that all that exists is a form of mind, so that there is no distinction between thought and existence.[8] Or one may, like French philosopher René Descartes (1596-1650), be a dualist and make some sharp distinction between mind and body and the material and spiritual universe (Descartes 1988)—a type of dualism usually known as "Cartesian dualism."

How one views the universe will affect how one views the idea of God and how a God relates to the universe. If one thinks all that exists is a form of mind or spirit stuff, then one may opt for pantheism, identifying God with the universe, seeing everything as part of God and God in everything.[9] Physicist Fritjof Capra, who emphasizes the basic energy aspect of the universe, has viewed quantum mechanics as a rediscovery of the Hindu god Shiva, the lord of the cosmic dance of creation and destruction, in which matter has no substance but consists of a perpetual dynamic and rhythmic gyration of energy (Capra 1983). If, however, one emphasizes the universe in its aspect of matter, it is going to be difficult to find place for the idea of God, and one may view ideas of God held by others in materialistic terms, rejecting them as impossible. This was the case with zoologist and philosopher Ernst Haeckel (1834-1919), who posited a single substance universe manifesting itself as matter and energy. Although he rejected materialism, using the term "spirit" to mean "energy," he ended up with a kind of natural, pantheistic, deterministic universe that, despite his religious attitude to nature, was closer to materialism than he realized. Human consciousness was a natural evolutionary product, and the idea of an actually transcendent God he described as a "gaseous vertebrate," an impossible notion (Desmond & Moore 1991, 543; Haeckel 1901). An extreme form of materialistic view can be found in the work of Erich von Daniken where the notion of God is materialized as a non-divine being, Daniken concluding from his archaeological and anthropological investigations that God was an astronaut visiting the earth (Daniken 1969). This type of view also occurs in the Raelian new religious movement, its founder, Claude Vorhilhon (Rael), declaring that in 1973 extra-terrestrials visiting earth revealed to him that the human race had been founded by the Elohim mentioned in the Bible, who were in fact scientifically minded extra-terrestrials. Raelian Tora Blackman underlined this explanation of the idea of God by declaring in a TV interview (WIN Australia 2004) that 2004 was the international year of atheism and that the myth of God was over.

If one is a Cartesian dualist, it is possible to make distinctions between God and the universe, and of course here, too, there are a number of positions. There is deism, where God is outside the universe and lets it go its way after initially starting it. There is also theism, where God has some kind of an ongoing relation with the universe. The universe may be seen as emanating from God, and God can be seen as relating personally to individuals and communities. With polytheism, there are, of course, many gods, and these are related to the universe in terms of how the people in question view its shape.[10] In Christianity, as we saw earlier, God can thus be said to be transcendent, above and beyond the world, and immanent, also in the world in some way. Important here, when we are considering Christianity, is how the person concerned views the universe in relation to the assumptions underlying the Christian tradition. As Peter Singer points out, Hegel has been classed as an atheist, as a pantheist, and as a panentheist (Singer 1983, 81-83). Yet people may have been unclear how Hegel viewed God and the universe because he was attempting to describe the universe in non-dualistic terms. Certainly the philosopher Leibniz experiences difficulties with his idea of the universe and his attempt to relate it to the Christian dualistic model. For Leibniz saw the world as made of one stuff, mind or spiritual stuff, and this stuff consisted of an infinite number of monads or spiritual energy points. His universe was arranged in a hierarchy of monads, with God as the top monad from whom the universe emanated after its initial start by God. God here is thus outside the whole process as cause and originator. Leibniz tried to unite Christian concepts with his description of the universe, but one can detect his struggle to do so. Leibniz thought that there was pre-existence and survival on this earth after death, but his one stuff system of monads is not conducive to the concept of individual life after death in heaven (Ross 1984, 106-08).

A variant of dualism is presented to us by physicist and pastor John Polkinghorne. For Polkinghorne, the world possesses a dual-aspect monism, the world being of one stuff, but irreducible to pure matter or mind, which should be seen as complementary poles of the single stuff. Polkinghorne, like many others, rejects Cartesian dualism because it fails adequately to explain how mind and body interact. For Polkinghorne, dual-aspect monism solves the problem (Polkinghorne 1996a, 60, 70; Polkinghorne 1988, 71-72; Polkinghorne 1989, 26). Given this picture, however, it is difficult to see how God can be actually transcendent (as well as immanent) as he is in Polkinghorne's view. How does God avoid being embodied in the physical universe, a view Polkinghorne rejects? (Crain 1997, 41-61; see Polkinghorne

1989, 19-23). What is the nature of the single stuff, and how far is the dual-aspect monism confined only to the mind and physical nature of humans? If this monistic one-stuff model extends to the entire universe, then how does God fit into the picture? Steven Crain raises this issue, and he compares Arthur Peacocke's model of the universe with Polkinghorne's. For Peacocke, God interacts with the state of the universe as a whole, such a model making room for an actually transcendent God. Crain thus finds Peacocke's model in this respect more satisfactory than Polkinghorne's (Crain 1997, 55-56).[11] We need to note, however, that Polkinghorne speaks of "the multi-layered" reality we encounter, and he sees the mind of the creator God as being behind the scientific order of the universe. God is transcendentally other, as well as the ground of the cosmic process; he is the single ground of everything. Although God is immanent and interacts with the world, he is also "in his eternity" (Polkinghorne 1988, 56, 69; Polkinghorne 1989, 27, 31-33, 83; Polkinghorne 1996a, 112). So Polkinghorne definitely perceives God as actually transcendent as well as immanent. Yet given that Polkinghorne is looking for a "unified view of reality," his dual-aspect monism presents difficulties, since the dualism part seems to relate to humans and the world, not to God and the universe. Description of God's relation to things as author to a book or play is a useful analogy, but it is not very helpful philosophically, because it still does not tell us how God can relate to the universe if we have to do with a one-stuff model (Polkinghorne 1988, 69, 55). Either the monistic model must be given up where God is concerned, or else we need a definition of dualism that will properly accommodate God so that he can be clearly understood to be actually transcendent as well as immanent. For when Polkinghorne thinks a full creation concept requires both the idea of God's original act of creation and his continuous creativity, and when he sees the evolutionary universe as a world that God lets make itself, "the result of a divine letting-be," God interacting with creation but not overruling it, the nature of the interaction is not clear, even though he suggests such an interaction might take place by means of "information input" into the physical process of creation (Polkinghorne 1996b, 44-45; Polkinghorne 1994, 71).

Finally, in this section, it needs to be noted that there can be conceptual misunderstandings through use of terms such as "supernature,"

"existence," "being," and of course "transcendence" and "eternal life."
When there is discussion about God using these terms, it is not always
clear that both sides of a discussion understand the same things by
them when they use them. There can also be a conceptual vagueness
about such terms unless they are specifically clarified in relation to
the discussion in question. For example, the term "supernature" is
often defined as having to do with some area capable of manifesting
the supernatural, namely the agency of something above or beyond
the forces of nature and the ordinary process of cause and effect; we
have to do with something that cannot be explained by appealing
to natural laws or phenomena. Yet for Lyall Watson, "supernature"
has to do with "one vast, self-maintaining system," so that we are all
"part of Supernature." In the introduction to his book, Watson uses
"Supernature" as a term for "a host of happenings" between nature
and the supernatural. For Watson, the traditional view of supernature
and the supernatural as inexplicable by the "known forces of nature"
is inadequate, for "Supernature knows no bounds....it is nature with
all its flavors intact, waiting to be tasted." In a number of places in his
book (which includes much discussion of areas belonging to the field
of parapsychology), he takes events that might be deemed supernatural
in a more traditional understanding of the term and attempts to give
a possible natural explanation for them (Watson 1974, 20, 12, 205,
208, 210-12, 230).

Similarly, as we have seen, it is important to make clear what we
mean when we use the term "transcendence." For example, theology
lecturer Alister Kee, following the thought that for many people belief
in God had become impossible, attempted to identify "transcendence"
as a secular term: transcendence as the way of life able to take the individual beyond self-interest, a life like that of Jesus. The question of
God's existence Kee left on one side, since he thought that the word
"God" as a term indicating what he describes as "traditional theism"
would make Christianity impossible for people in contemporary
society if they had to presuppose the existence of God (Kee 1971;
Hoare 1972, 155-56).

"Existence" is also a difficult term and has been the subject of debate
and misunderstanding, not least in the ontological argument for God's
existence put forward by Anselm of Canterbury (1033-1109). A key

element of his most known argument turns on his assumption that it is more perfect to exist than not to exist, hence, God, since he is perfect, exists. Yet it has to be asked, as many have, whether "existence" is a predicate.—It is not clear that "a cow exists [is there] in Farmer Giles' meadow," is the same kind of statement as "the cow is fat." Thus it is important to consider exactly how a term is being used. Nor must we forget that translation can produce misunderstanding, as with the statement by the Danish thinker Søren Kierkegaard's pseudonym, Johannes Climacus, that "God does not exist, he is eternal." In English, we have the one word "exist" and "existence" for something that in Danish can occur as two different words. When Johannes Climacus states that God does not exist, he simply means that God does not exist in the way humans do, with a developmental history. He does not mean there is no God, for otherwise he would have used the Danish "er til" instead of "existere" (Kierkegaard 1992, 332).

Then there is the difficult word "Being," used by many, not least bishop Spong, who, as we have seen, follows Paul Tillich's use of the phrase "the Ground of Being" to describe God. Yet, as theologian John Macquarrie has pointed out, Tillich, in trying to avoid using a descriptor for God that could indicate him as an entity among other entities, gets himself into difficulties. When Tillich speaks of God as "being itself," or as the "ground of being," the term is used in two different senses, since "being itself" viewed as something ultimate cannot have a ground. Macquarrie also objects to Tillich's ambiguous application to God of the phrase "power of being" (Macquarrie 1971, 367, fn. 2). So Spong using Tillich's terminology, in the thought that this will give people a clearer idea of God, does not in fact improve the situation for others. Indeed, it might even be argued that he makes things worse, given that he also uses God terminology (e.g. "transcendence") that indicates "aboveness," despite his apparent reuse of the word.

One can therefore conclude that concerning claims about God's existence, one person's meat can be another's poison, or at least confusion, and that when writing books indicating or denying God's existence, the writers not only need to take more care with their use of terminology, they also need to avoid assuming their outlook on God is necessarily superior to the views of others. Since the question of God's existence is a metaphysical one, atheists are free to disbelieve, while believers are equally free to believe, especially if they have reasons for thinking their belief is justified. It also always needs to be remembered that any description of God's position, from "above" to the unclear and rather ambiguous "ground of being" (with its linguistic connotation of being below us), may be totally unlike the state of affairs as it really is. On the assumption that there is a God, and a sphere of existence corresponding to an actual transcendence, we cannot know that it makes any sense to apply spatial designations to the situation. In our finite state, and with our limited knowledge, we are thrown back on the concepts that can be expressed in the various languages of the world. Given this, it then surely does not matter that one person thinks of God in heaven above, and another thinks of God as the bedrock of everything, and so on. Nor, in my view, has another person any right to decide on behalf of another exactly what picture that person has in mind when using a particular concept, or that he or she ought to conform to some other concept in the name of the imprecise notion of "modernity." Having said this, it is perfectly fair that the non-believer or anyone else considers statements put forward by believers and tries to understand what might be meant by them. This also, of course, applies to descriptions and pictures of God.

(e) Descriptions and Pictures of God

We have now arrived at the second question about God, namely which descriptions or pictures of God are morally or factually acceptable. Again, we need constantly to bear in mind that any picture of God, however elevated it may be, is going to be a human construct. Yet unless we are able, like the author of *The Cloud of Unknowing*, to avoid conceptualizing God at all, it is likely that the believer will have some special idea, symbol, or concept of God even though, as in Islamic mosques, there may be no religious pictures or images, whereas Christianity varies between having as few as possible (even none) in its churches to having many.[12] Given that some pictures of God impinge directly upon community through religious traditions, we need to ask ourselves how far those outside those traditions are justified in condemning them. When biologist Richard Dawkins likens God to Father Christmas and the tooth fairy (Stannard 1993, 4; see Spong 1999, 204), he appears to think that believers have in mind a picture of God as an old man with a white beard, and that they also see God as a benevolent giver of anything asked for. While Dawkins is clearly incorrect if he imagines this is how everyone pictures God, is he wrong to attack the notion of God as giver of anything asked for? If this is what Dawkins had in mind when making his comment, one has to agree with him, as would most serious believers in God, that the idea of God as a benevolent super-giver, there to supply us with anything we want, is an unhealthy one.

One can recall the "pact of plenty" that missionary-evangelist T.L. Osborn wanted people to make with God through his postal evangelical paper *Special Digest*.—Osborn, who seems to have regarded himself as divinely sponsored by God, urged people to have faith, save up five pounds each month, mailing the money to the organization with a prayer slip on which the individual ticked relevant need boxes on the list. Osborn and his associates would then pray that the person's most urgent need of the month would be met by divine miracle. The list of needs included health, joy and salvation, but there was also a heavy material emphasis, with many case examples given in the paper to show that God was prospering thousands of people financially through the pact.— Although there was a warning that the end of the world was coming and people should not let themselves be overcome by greed, selfishness, and materialism, they were encouraged to think of God as one who would give people all kinds of financial and other benefits. In this picture, God was not only a super-giver of anything asked for, he also seemed fussy about his mediator, who, in this case, seemed to be Osborn and his associates rather than Jesus Christ (Osborn Foundation 1972, 2, 7, 10, 14-16, 12). This is not to say that it is wrong for believers to bring needs and problems to God, or that Osborn was wrong to the extent that he encouraged them to bring needs to God, but clearly prayer consisting of making demands, or asking for material goods in a self-centred, acquisitive frame of mind, seems totally inappropriate and foreign to the life of the spirit.

Yet does it matter if some people do have a picture of God as a benevolent father figure (or a benevolent mother figure) if the picture is free from materialistic self-seeking on the part of the believer? Kierkegaard deals with this issue in *Concluding Unscientific Postscript* (Kierkegaard 1992, 201) where he describes two people: a Christian who has the dogmatically correct Christian picture of God, but "prays in untruth" in Church, and the pagan who prays passionately to an image of an idol. He asserts that the pagan is praying in truth to God even though he is worshipping an idol, whereas the Christian may be praying to the true God, but he is "praying in untruth." The point here is that the Christian in question is merely paying lip-service to intellectual concepts that mean little, or perhaps nothing, to him, whereas the pagan is a totally committed believer seeking God, even though he may think God dwells on earth as the idol, or is identical with the idol. The tenor of Kierkegaard's writings views the godly life as ideally one of selfless commitment to God and others, following the example of the New Testament Jesus. So for Kierkegaard, anyone praying to God self-centredly or indifferently, could never have a correct picture of the nature of God. The same point is made by C.S. Lewis in his Narnia story, *The Last Battle* (Lewis 1964, 146-49), where, in the afterlife, the Calormene Emeth, who has worshipped and served the god Tash all his life, encounters Aslan, the true God. Since he has been brought up to view Aslan as a false god, Emeth is troubled, but Alsan tells him that even though Emeth thought he was serving Tash, in fact he was really serving Aslan, since all vile deeds and cruelties done by people, even if done in the name of Aslan, belong to the service of Tash, whereas all good deeds and acts of unselfishness belong to the service of Aslan. Here, of course, we face the vexed question of which moral code is to be used to judge what is moral and godly service and what is not. C.S. Lewis attempts to answer this question to a certain extent by giving a list of examples of what he sees as universal natural moral law, to be found in cultural and religious traditions all over the world (Lewis 1978, esp. 49-59). Philosopher Louis Pojman deals with the question by analysing ethical relativism, showing that one can take note of the insights such a position provides but refute the validity of ethical relativism (Pojman 1995, 29-37). Major world religions of course also provide codes of behaviour for believers, and it is safe to say that things such as cruelty, murder, and totally self-centred acts would not be done by the genuinely godly believer, whereas acts of kindness, etc. would. A clear example here is that of the prison warden in the 1993 film *The Shawshank Redemption*, where the warden is apparently a deeply-committed, practising Christian, yet he is morally corrupt, even ready to stoop to arranging a murder when necessary to his interests.

It may be objected that, since different religions present us with different concepts of God or a divine God-source, not all of them can be factually true. I will enlarge upon this topic in the next chapter, but I will first consider the problem briefly here. As we have already seen (see also Goulder & Hick 1983, ch. 2, esp. 31-32; Spong 1999, 47, 58), people think differently about God, and those committed to the various religious traditions are likely to think about God in ways belonging to their traditions, however varied their individual God concepts may be. We have also discussed the metaphysical barrier preventing us from arriving at the true state of affairs about God and the universe. When Gandhi, however, sees it as natural that people's conceptions of God would vary according to the experience of each person (Gandhi 1958, 79), are we into a different situation? This depends on what we mean by "experience." If this is the cultural experience of practising a religion, then it will not be surprising that a Hindu thinks of a Hindu deity, whereas a Christian associates Jesus with the God-concept. Yet what are we to make of reports of near-death experiences, where people report encounters with Hindu deities, Christ, or some figure or figures from their particular religion? (Patterson 2002a). Are we to dismiss such reports out of hand as hallucinations, or is there another possible explanation? I will deal with this question in the next chapter. Here, I will conclude by pointing out that the debates of former times as to which religion had the correct, factual, idea of God, can be seen as conceptually impossible to decide because of the metaphysical barrier. Also, as Max Charlesworth has pointed out (Charlesworth 1997, esp. 23-50), we probably should be starting from the fact of the diversity of religions and view any religion as an active response to the divine. Thus, fragmentation of particular religions into various groups and sects can then be seen as differing interpretations that have developed out of the original mainstream religion, and the need to try to "convert" someone to a different idea of God solely on grounds of factual truth is unnecessary and inappropriate.

Chapter Two
Communication of the Divine—
Communication with the Divine

I n this chapter I will consider some indicators of an actual divine transcendence. Then I will deal with some conceptual difficulties concerning descriptions of the self. After this I will discuss the question of religious authority, where alleged manifestation of the divine to humans is concerned, and the response of humans to such authority. Finally, I will consider the forms in which the divine is claimed to manifest itself, and the question of prayer as communication with the divine.

(a) Indicators of an Actual Divine Transcendence?

We have seen clearly that science cannot answer metaphysical questions with any certainty. Similarly arguments for God's existence, or against God's existence, while clarifying some issues (see Hick 1990, chs. 2 & 3), cannot provide certainty either, especially since we are trapped within the constraints of language and of our assumptions. The believer is thus referred to the area of beliefs and faith. Yet there has always been the factor of people's religious experience of God or the divine, as can be seen from the spiritual literature in the different religious traditions. Besides this, there are contemporary accounts of people's religious experiences. Zoologist/biologist Alister Hardy (1896-1985) did pioneering work in this area when he collected together a variety of reports of religious experiences of all kinds and started the Religious Experience Research Unit at Manchester College, Oxford in 1969. In his book, *The Spiritual Nature of Man* (Hardy 1979), he attempted to classify various elements of reported religious experience that he had gathered together in intensive surveys. Another biologist, David Hay, continuing Hardy's work, discussed the research in this area, finding that reports of encounters with some non-physical power beyond the individual self were far more widespread than had previously been thought, and that the experiences reported also included accounts by people outside any religious tradition (Hay 1987 & 1990).[13]

While the evidence put forward by the collectors of accounts of religious experience cannot be dismissed, it is problematic how far it can be used to indicate an actual sphere of transcendence and an actually transcendent God or divine power. Hardy very much wished to combat materialism, seeing a science of theology as a path to overtly regaining human spirituality in an age of materialistic secularism. Yet, as J.E. Platt points out (Platt 1973, 507-13 esp. 511-13), a natural history of religious experience indicates a naturalistic view of the entire universe, so that religious experience must somehow be incorporated (along with the field of parapsychology), into the natural world. Hardy, a professed Darwinist, attempted to deal with this question by positing the possibility of a dualism of material and mental/spiritual elements of the universe. Unfortunately, however, Hardy's dualism seems to rest on a confusion between the idea of an actual transcendence and that which is non-material. Hardy would like to avoid philosophy and metaphysics, but does not realize that if he would wish to view religious experience as being that of an actual transcendence of some kind, he cannot escape the metaphysical barrier. If one does not discuss parapsychological and religious experience solely within the framework of the sciences like Lyall Watson—Watson, like Hardy, also includes evolutionary development in his thinking (Hardy 1966, 34-36; Watson 1974, 286-87)—then at some point one has to make a personal decision based on a leap for or against actual transcendence of some kind and/or God or a divine power. If one takes the leap against an actual transcendence, then, as Alan Keightley has pointed out (Keightley 1976, ch. 5, esp. 125-26), talk of God can become an expression of values. If one opts for an actual transcendence of some kind, then God talk for the believer has reference to facts.[14] For a natural scientist, however, there is the further option of attempting to translate "God facts" into scientific facts. One can try to give apparent religious experience of actual transcendence a natural explanation of some kind. Yet, as Platt shows (Platt 1973, 513), while science can legitimately be used in relation to religious experience (for example, in the scientific gathering of accounts of such experience), it cannot be extended into an area beyond its scope. The scientist who sets out to give reports of experiences of God and the divine a purely scientific explanation has done so on the basis of an assumption or belief that there is no God or an actual transcendence.

Apart from the problem of the metaphysical barrier, it is clearly extremely difficult for science to handle religious experience other than by documenting reports. Even the attempt to classify individual accounts as types of such experience may be difficult, since, as we noted earlier, it is not possible to take the experience out of a person in its raw state and compare it in a laboratory with other individual raw state experiences. In addition, one cannot repeat the individual experience, even though an individual may report several such experiences in his or her life. Also, as Rosalind Heywood has pointed out with reference to parapsychological experience (Heywood 1971, chs. XIV-XVI), such experiences occur whenever they occur, whereas when trying to evoke such experiences in the laboratory, the somewhat boring and repetitive nature of the experiments (e.g. card-guessing), seems to act against the manifestation of the experiences one is trying to study.

Finally, there is a problem for those considering whether a God or actual transcendence exists, namely that some have clear religious experiences that seem to indicate God or the divine, whereas others, as we noted with British pastor Michael Goulder, do not. Given that God is traditionally alleged to have all the positive moral qualities, including being a just God, one may well wonder why that God limits the experiences, or why some seem to have many and others never have any at all. I have two suggestions concerning this question. First, I think the more one uses the conceptualizing part of the mind, the less likelihood there is of having such experiences at that time. That is, when I am thinking about something, even if I am thinking about arguments for or against the existence of God, I have taken a step back from existential contact with the world. Agreeing with Kierkegaard in his *Concluding Unscientific Postscript* (Kierkegaard 1992, 307-18), I think one abstracts from existence in order to consider issues. One has also necessarily set boundaries concerning the object of thought. Although I have taken a step back into myself, so to speak, it is not in the sense of religious meditation or contemplation, where one existentially tries to break free of conceptualizing (Underhill 1914, chs. IV, VII, VIII).

Second, we are all individuals, and it is not impossible that some of us are better constructed than others to receive spontaneous religious experiences. As an analogy, I will take the ability to do mathematics. Contrary to what many think, not everyone is able to do them or do much in the way of arithmetic, and this is because the person in question has a different type of mind. I can here speak from my own experience, in that despite my interest in the subject, I have always been totally incapable of reading the language of mathematics, and have great trouble with anything set up as figures for calculation. Thus, when I philosophize about mathematics, the philosophizing is always totally devoid of mathematics or figures in any conceptual form. Stephen Hawking, on the other hand, oozes mathematical ability. Thus, when he writes mathematical formula, I believe that he has done the calculations and that mathematics have a reality. Indeed, if I were to conclude from my very innumerate state that mathematics did not really exist, and that Hawking and other mathematicians were somehow deceived, I would be totally wrong from their perspective, even though I am incapable of the actual mathematical experience and must trust that they are really doing the mathematics that effect so much in our lives. Hence those who conclude, from not having had any kind of religious or even parapsychological experience, that God and actual transcendence cannot possibly exist, and that this world is all we have, are making an assumption based only on the example of their own experience. Of course it can always be suggested that those who do have such experiences are deceived or hallucinating, but this tends to be a weak objection where such people are level-headed and describe such experiences as overwhelming, definitely indicating a reality other than themselves.

Yet it is here that we are inevitably thrown back on belief and faith, and also, of course, on cultural and other factors that may incline us either in the direction of belief or of disbelief. So before discussing claims that an actually transcendent God relates to humans, and that humans can and do have a relationship with God, I would like first to discuss some conceptual difficulties concerning descriptions of the self.

(b) Some Conceptual Difficulties Concerning Descriptions of the Self

It is not surprising that how one views the nature of the human self is dependent on how one views the basic nature of the universe, whether or not one has reflected on one's underlying assumptions in this direction. If one sees the universe in terms of energy/matter particles, then mind or consciousness will, as we have seen, be interpreted in relation to the material body; one will identify the mind in some way with the physical body as all of a piece, or at least take an approach that bypasses the possibility of making a mind/body division. A Cartesian dualist, on the other hand, will be open to making a distinction between the body and mind or consciousness. Not that a person necessarily starts from conscious considerations about the universe and arrives at a particular conclusion about the nature of the human self. It is merely self-evident that conscious or unconscious assumptions made by the Cartesian dualist do not fit a purely materialistic/physicalist understanding of the universe, just as the physicalist will find no place for the assumptions of the Cartesian dualist.[15]

Thought about the subject of human consciousness and how we relate to the universe has been confused by the factor of different concepts handed down to us. When we examine writings or hear people talk about the human self and how it may relate to God in this world or after death, a number of terms may be used, without those using them necessarily being clear about the origin and original meaning of the terms. When one hears people talk of "body and mind," "body and soul" and "body, mind and spirit," the terms are often used to make a distinction between the bodily side of the self as organism and the inner self. "Mind" may be used to indicate the intellectual, creative and emotive aspects of the inner self, whereas the terms "soul" and "spirit" carry religious connotations and indicate something more, as C.S. Lewis attempted to show when he attempted to clarify the meaning of the terms "spirit" and "spiritual" (Lewis 1947, 203-07; Lewis 1974, 73-77). "Psyche" of course is also used of the self in relation to thought about the psychological profile of a person, though it may sometimes be used to suggest also the spiritual nature of a person, as in "psychic expos."

Not everyone is clear, however, that Hebrew and Greek thought in the Bible lie behind these concepts. In the Old Testament, "soul" was "nephesh" or the vapour of life in the blood, whereas the Greek world supplied "psyche" as the notion of a "divine spark" in a person. "Spirit" in the Old Testament ("ruach") signifies air in motion, the idea of the breath of God, and of communication with God. In the New Testament, spirit ("pneuma") signifies God as pure spirit, also human faculties given a person by God, and finally, the idea of the whole person in relation to God. Also to be found are the terms "flesh" ("basar" in the Old Testament, "sarx" in the New Testament), signifying human physical nature, seen as weak in comparison with God. Finally, "body" occurs in the New Testament as "soma," both the dead and the living body, with the suggestion of continuance between this life and the next. Behind these terms lie differences between Old and New Testament thought. In the Old Testament, immortality consisted of long life in the land if one were morally faithful to Yahweh. The dead went to Sheol, that is, into the ground where the dead were cut off from God. In the period between the Testaments, ideas of life after death arose, with notions of hell for the ungodly and heaven for the godly. In the New Testament, the Pharisees believed in resurrection of the body, and resurrection is a major New Testament theme. Paul, in a letter to the Corinthians (I Cor. 15 v. 35-44), dismisses the question of what kind of resurrection body the dead have. He asserts that in life it is a physical body, but it is raised as a spiritual one. There are thus notions of physical and spiritual bodies in the New Testament. The resurrection body of Jesus seems to be both physical and spiritual. On the one hand he is physical enough to eat and be touched after death, and on the other he is able to come through locked doors and to vanish (Luke, ch. 24; John, ch. 20).

When Christianity encountered the Greek world, it encountered different ideas about the self. In Greek thought, "soul" was defined in a dualistic opposition to "body," whereas in Hebrew thinking there was no dualism. In the Greek mystery-cult of Orphism (see also the earlier dialogues of Plato), dualism between soul and body is emphasized. The soul belongs to the divine, eternal realm, and is the undying, indestructible part of a person, confined to the body during life. Salvation of the soul is the release of the immortal part from the mortal part. In Plato, the "eternal" is accessed through the mind, and is part of an eternal realm of eternal truths and concepts. The Hebrew view of the person is thus of an animated body, whereas the Greek view sees a human being as an incarnated soul.

Given this background, it is hardly surprising that it is difficult to speak coherently of the self in terms of life after death or in relation to a transcendent God or eternity. In the Christian tradition there have been those who have insisted upon a physical resurrection of a person after death, and those who have emphasized the resurrection body in spiritual terms. The notion of "soul," seen as something immortal, thus fits in somewhat uneasily with ideas of resurrection. This can be seen very clearly in the Christian catechism written by Nikolai Edinger Balle (1744-1816), a Danish bishop whose catechism, based on Luther's Lesser Catechism, has a chapter on the final state of a person (Balle 1791, ch. 8). Attempting to deal with the question (in the Christian tradition) of what happens to those who die before the second coming of Christ, Balle states that at death the human soul, since it is immortal already, goes immediately to heaven or hell according to the person's moral behaviour in life. The body will be resurrected physically on the last day of the world and reunited with the soul. Those still alive on earth on the last day will not die, in the sense of being separated from their souls for a time, but will undergo immediate change into the resurrected state. After this universal resurrection of the living and the dead Jesus judges everyone and it is publicly revealed who are confirmed as participators in heaven and who are condemned to eternal punishment. Balle thus attempts to unite two different ideas about life after death, namely immortality and resurrection.[16]

John Polkinghorne attempts to deal with the question of life after death through his dual-aspect monism. He thinks we are psychosomatic unities, with the soul as the information-bearing pattern of the body. He sees the pattern as subject to dissolution at death, but thinks that one's pattern can be remembered by God and recreated in some new environment in God's ultimate act of resurrection (Polkinghorne 1996a, 95-101 esp. 100, see 53-74). The difficulty with this description is that on the one hand, it cannot free itself from the problems of Polkinghorne's view that we discussed earlier, and on the other, we can see the same attempt as Balle's to accommodate different concepts from the Christian tradition in one explanation.

The influence of the Christian tradition, with its Hebraic and Greek elements concerning the nature of human beings (coupled with the effect of Descartes' dualism between mind and the material world—though he also speaks of the soul and its immortality), has thus made it extremely difficult to talk about what a person's situation after death might or might not be. Nor has it made the idea of relating to God and eternity in this life any easier. As John Hick has pointed out, after World War II, there was a cultural rejection of belief in personal immortality, and he sees this as due to a general assumption that one should believe only what one experiences and what the sciences indicate is truth (Hick 1976, chs. 4 & 5, esp. 92-93; see Hick 1990, chs. 10 & 11; Toynbee 1968).—It is therefore not surprising that philosopher D.Z. Phillips (Phillips 1970, chs. 1-3, esp. 38, 49) has treated beliefs about immortality, resurrection, and eternal life as subjective expressions of the state of the soul (thus retaining a temporal concept of eternal life) even though he does not think he will meet his loved ones after death. For Peter Atkins (Atkins 1994, 35) "the only immortal soul man has is the lasting impression he makes on other men's minds."—Since Hick wrote his book, there has, of course, been an increasing emphasis on new age religions and ideas of spirituality, but this does not seem to have improved the situation overmuch. To confuse things further, interest in eastern religions has encouraged a number of people in the Christian church to include reincarnation in their Christian beliefs. Indeed, some have wanted to include reincarnation as a part of the basis of Christian faith (Kirkegaard 1999; Bryld 1999; Holmgaard 1999; Kristeligt Dagblad 2004). On the other hand there are those who take the idea of resurrection in a totally material and secular sense, and do not mind paying to have their bodies (or their heads, if they think this is where their self resides) frozen down in the hope of being revived some day and in some way by science (Patterson 2002b).

Finally, we should not forget the effect of the psychology of Sigmund Freud (1856-1939) and Carl Jung (1875-1961), who left us the concepts of ego, super-ego and id, and the collective unconscious. Indeed, Freud has been seen as fathering the idea of the unconscious mind, even though others before him had talked about unconscious mental processes (Storr 1989; Stevens 1994). Yet one can ask to what extent an individual's mind is unconscious. How far do we accept psychological concepts from authority figures and the culture as basic facts rather than possibilities, although exploring the human mind is not on a par with finding out biological facts about life forms?

We are thus left with a basic problem concerning the self, namely, that we have inherited a multiplicity of conceptual descriptions of the self from our culture—which is why it may not be terribly helpful when John Spong speaks of "a divine presence called spirit within us" or of Jesus as "a spirit person" (Spong 1999, 117)—yet at the same time, as we have seen before, it is not possible to lay out individual minds (as opposed to brains) in the laboratory, in order to see how far they can be compared. Also, each person's attempt at a personal description of his or her mind or self, to the extent the person is able to assess it, must be expressed through the language of that person's culture and the framework of that person's beliefs, not to mention through the understanding of the one hearing the description. We can therefore expect a variety of personal assessments varying from atheistic or neutral models, to those that, like Kierkegaard's dynamic relational model, assume the existence of an actually transcendent God to whom the self needs to relate in order to become a complete person (Kierkegaard 1980).

(c) On Manifestations of an Actually Transcendent Divinity

For the sake of ease of discussion, I will continue to speak of an actually transcendent God or divinity, setting aside the fact that we cannot know for certain scientifically, the state of affairs that prevails in the universe concerning God's existence. Thus we are here dealing with belief in an actual transcendence, backed up so far by people's claims to have had religious experiences. In the history of Christianity, and of course religion generally, claims have been made to specific revelations of the divine. This type of revelation may be directly from God to an individual. Such revelations may be the advent of a divine figure to the world, as in the case of Christianity, or it may be that an individual will receive a communication leading to the foundation of a religion, as in the case of the revelation to Muhammed of the Koran. Or someone may be commissioned to preach a religion, as was the case with the apostle Paul. Finally there are divine messages to individuals about various matters. With all these types of revelation, it has to be asked what factual credence one should give to claims made by individuals that they have received some kind of communication from God.

With revelations belonging to major religions, it can be argued that the life and message of the founders of such religions speak for themselves. In other words, one can at least assess the quality of the life and message to a certain extent, before committing oneself to the religion in question.[17] What of specific messages from God, however, that may seem to be of a dubious nature? In the Old Testament, the story of the test of Abraham, God's request that Abraham sacrifice his son, has been endlessly written about and debated. In the Old Testament, it was, of course, only a test, for God had the ram in readiness. Yet Aldous Huxley points out that "by no means all inspirations are divine," and tells us of the case of a pious Anabaptist who thought God had inspired him to decapitate his brother as an Isaac, the latter also being convinced of the truth of God's wish. Hence the assenting brother was duly beheaded in the presence of a large religious congregation (Gen. ch. 22; Huxley 1986, 85-86).

Søren Kierkegaard (1813-1855) had good cause to deal with the issue of revelation. In 1843, he had written *Fear and Trembling*, specifically dealing with the case of Abraham and Isaac, and showing it to be what he called "a teleological suspension" of the ordinary ethical for the sake of a higher religious ethic. Such a case could not be humanly justified, since in no way was the intended sacrifice for the sake of anyone in the community. All Abraham could do was to venture in faith, trusting to God's goodness, or leave it (Kierkegaard 1983; Mooney 1991). In 1843, however, a contemporary of Kierkegaard's, pastor Adolph Adler (1812-1869), published a book of sermons (Adler 1843) which he prefaced with what he claimed to be a revelation from Jesus. This case presented a problem for Kierkegaard, since Christianity was founded on a revelation, and he had just dealt with the case of Abraham and Isaac. Kierkegaard could not avoid having to explain in some way the difference between accepted revelations and the case of pastor Adler.

Adler was suspended by the Church authorities and then pensioned off because of his claim, but Kierkegaard felt something more was needed.

Adler had claimed to have had a flash of illumination one night, followed by his hearing "a hideous noise," after which Jesus told him to burn the philosophical material Adler had published on Hegel, and to keep to the Bible in future. Adler was also told to write down the words of the revelation that he then published in the preface to his book of sermons. The revelation consisted of a few lines in which evil is described as originating in the world through "human thought becoming wrapped up in itself." Kierkegaard, in a letter to his brother (June 29, 1843) describes Adler, who visited Copenhagen and Kierkegaard at this time, as an able scholar, but rather worked up (Kierkegaard 1978, 155-56). We also learn from Kierkegaard that Adler ascribed to Kierkegaard the status of John the Baptist as forerunner to himself, who was a messiah by virtue of his revelation. He read sections of his book to Kierkegaard in an ordinary voice, but also some in a peculiar whispering voice. When Kierkegaard felt obliged to say he did not see anything new in Adler's material, Adler said he would come back again later and read it all in the whispering voice, when the revelation would become clear to Kierkegaard.

Kierkegaard was fascinated by the case of Adler, since Kierkegaard had previously said one must choose either to accept or reject a revelation on the basis of belief. He thought that, in the case of such a claim, someone might have a genuine revelation, but that it could also be the case of someone putting on an act for some reason. When he encountered the Adler case, Kierkegaard realized that of course there was also the possibility of mental disturbance. So while he continued to think one could not objectively prove or disprove a revelation claim, he allowed that one could first look at the circumstances surrounding the alleged revelation. This led Kierkegaard to write what became his posthumously published *Book on Adler* (Kierkegaard 1998a). In this book, he develops several criteria that can be used in order to test the circumstances surrounding a revelation claim. First, he considers the personal circumstances surrounding such a claim. Is there any mental confusion or disturbance in the words or behaviour of the individual? Second, Kierkegaard wants to know whether the alleged revelation really brings anything new when one compares its content with the presuppositions of the established religion or order of things. Third, Kierkegaard insists on consistency in the claims made. While he sees nothing wrong if an individual changes the description of the alleged revelation event, thus retracting the original description, Kierkegaard points out that one cannot simultaneously ascribe totally different claims to the same event as if there is no difference in the descriptions. Finally, Kierkegaard expects the individual receiving a revelation to become a godly, altruistic person, a christlike figure, at least from the time of having the revelation. This last criterion is so important for Kierkegaard that he even uses it as a test of the Christian revelation: If Christ had triumphed through meddlesomeness and cunning political rhetoric, then he would not have been genuinely the messiah and Christianity would not have been Christianity (Kierkegaard 1998a, fn. 159; see Watkin 1992, 27-40; Evans 2000, 48-67).

While Kierkegaard's criteria were helpful with respect to Adler and can be extremely helpful in identifying "religious" claims stemming from fraud and craziness, there are still some tricky questions left to answer. Kierkegaard makes a watertight distinction between genius and apostleship in his book, based on his sharp, dualistic distinction between immanence and an actual sphere of transcendence. Similarly, he derives his notion of religious authority and genuine altruism solely from this distinction. Yet while some instances correspond to this distinction, it is hard to see how a William Blake or an Emanuel Swedenborg fit into the scheme. Second, it is not always easy to draw a sharp line between what constitutes religiousness and what craziness. One must also ask how far someone suffering from mental illness must be excluded from the possibility of having an authentic revelation. Third, a truly humble and godly person might be genuinely mistaken in some way about some revelation claim. So while Kierkegaard is correct about the weight of responsibility entailed in assessing such claims, there are a number of grey transition areas that have to be taken into consideration.

(d) Forms in which Divinity Manifests Itself

We saw in the previous chapter that people in different religious traditions claim that the divine has manifested itself to them in figures from their own tradition. Setting aside here claims made by people who are clearly mentally disturbed, and who would thus not meet Kierkegaard's criteria, what are we to make of such claims made by sober, stable people, given that many religions have claimed to be the one true faith? In addition to this, there is the fact that a divine figure from a particular religious tradition does not manifest itself in the same manner to people in that tradition.

My response to the first question is that, on the assumption that there is a divine power behind everything, one can scarcely expect that power to be less intelligent than humans. Indeed, God has been called "omniscient" and "omnipotent," much to the dismay of those claiming that a good God could not be good, possessing these qualities and apparently doing nothing about the evils of the world (see Spong 1999, 6-7). While it is true that attempts at theodicy—for example, that God permits evil and suffering in order to maintain human freedom and an environment conducive to soul-making (Kierkegaard 1967-78, II, F-K, entry 1251; Hick 1968), and that the believer can view personal suffering as material to be used positively for others in some way, even as prayer for someone or some situation, or as an aspect of the God-relationship (Laurentin 1979, 188-90; Weil 1963, 101)—at best give only a partial response to the the problem of evil and suffering where an omnipotent and omniscient God is concerned, the fact that the ultimate answer lies (just as does the fact of the existence of good and good things in the world) on the other side of the metaphysical barrier should not cause us to reject the possibility of an intelligent divine power behind things. Humans who are good teachers know that it is important to start from where people are—from what they understand, and to teach by first finding common ground. Otherwise the pupils or students just do not understand what it is one is trying to communicate to them. Søren Kierkegaard did just this through his authorship, in which he wished to make clear to people what it means to become a Christian. He believed that one could not communicate fresh ideas to people, especially if they were set in their ways, by making direct assertions. Hence he used his tactic of "indirect communication" of ideas, socratically presenting different discursive characters through his pseudonymous works and "without authority."[18] It therefore should not be surprising that God would be manifested through various divinities appropriate to the presuppositions and beliefs of the person in question. To take a rather comic example here, when some photographers wished to come close to Tasmanian devils in order to take pictures, they dressed themselves up as kangaroos in order to appear as something familiar to the animals they were photographing. The taking of pictures as an activity would have been the same however they dressed themselves, but only the kangaroo dress was appropriate to the situation.

This line of thinking can also be applied to the fact that a divine figure from a particular religious tradition is not manifested in the same manner to people in that tradition. For example, many in the Roman Catholic world have claimed to have had a visitation from the Virgin Mary, but the descriptions of the figure are very varied. For example, Bernadette's Virgin was a beautiful blue-eyed girl, the same height as Bernadette, wearing a white dress with a blue girdle (Laurentin 1979, 177, 120, see 31-34, 195). The Virgin of the Curé d'Ars was a lady of middle height wearing jewels, a decorated dress and a crown. The Virgin of Fatima was a lady all in white in a simple tunic (Ghéon 1946, 219-21; Walsh 1954, 50-51; see Zimdars-Swartz 1991). To be historically correct, however, the mother of Jesus ought to have been brown-eyed with skin colour and clothing appropriate to the Middle East. In addition to this are claims made by people to have seen metaphysical figures such as archangels. The most well-known example is that of the visitation of the archangels Michael and Gabriel to Joan of Arc and her encounters with other saints, some of whom were non-historical figures (Sackville-West 1990, 49, 53-54, 285, 293-97). All these examples can be explained in terms of the divine manifesting itself in figures and forms belonging to a person's background and religious tradition.

Yet what are we to make of the example of the atheistic Hans Post, former Nazi and member of the SS, who came to understand the entire Nazi ideology for what it was and to reject it? Hans, in the account of his life, describes several encounters with a figure he calls the archangel Michael, going from the first encounter in 1946 to his last in 1989 in Australia. Michael appeared to Hans immaculately dressed in the uniform of a highly decorated officer in the SS. He claimed to have met Hans before on the steps of a brothel. In the next encounter, he gave Hans some good advice that enabled him to survive the ordeal of the prison camp. He appeared again in 1955 to reassure Hans that he would be rescued from being trapped in a mine. When Hans was purchasing a property in Australia in 1989, Michael again turned up to tell him accurately where to bore a well. A curious feature of Michael was that he seemed to age along with Hans, who initially put the manifestation down to being only a product of his subconscious mind. Interestingly, when Hans was on board ship with his first wife Lydi, Michael again came and approved Hans' decision to leave Germany, but this time Lydi felt the presence of someone, even though she could not see Michael (Post 2002, 205-08, 281, 381, 389-92). I think in this case we can still follow the same principle when we study Hans' past and find that his sense of ideality in relation to Nazism was particularly in relation to the idealism of the elite corps of which Hans was a member under Otto Skorzeny. Thus one should not associate atrocities with Hans' youthful picture of Nazism, even though he came to understand that the underlying ideology and associated actions were utterly odious. Given that Hans was an atheist, it is not surprising that he should experience a communication through something down-to-earth and in line with his initial picture of ideality. Nor need the fact that the manifestation came through Hans himself necessarily exclude an objective element in it. The same might be said of the Curé d'Ars' vision of the Virgin, since a Catharine Lassagne witnessed the vision and noted that the Curé was standing by the table with shining face and fixed glance. In short, just as ordinary communication between a teacher and student depends on the student having the mental and physical apparatus for appropriating what is said and making internal sense of it—a subjective element entering into the receiving of the communication—so, too, can one think that the divine could communicate itself in many ways, using the person's consciousness to shape the form of the communication. This is why Lyall Watson's objection concerning paranormal apparations that people see ghosts in clothes "as they or somebody else remembers them" (Watson 1974, 278) is irrelevant to such issues and cannot be used to dismiss the authenticity of such an experience.

That a religion should then appropriate someone's vision as part of that tradition is not surprising. We can see this happening in the case of Bernadette, where her respectful "Aquerò" [that thing] was later taken into the Roman Catholic tradition as a manifestation of the Virgin on the basis of Bernadette's report that the apparition said she was "the immaculate conception." That Bernadette did not immediately claim that the apparition was the Virgin of the immaculate conception surely lends a ring of objective truth to her account should anyone think that she was merely a young woman with an over-lively imagination (Laurentin 1979, 43, 48, 82-84). It is also interesting to consider that the words spoken by the vision, "Que soy era Immaculada Councepciou" [I am the immaculate conception], initially so puzzling to the clergy, might, if the patois word for "conception" had the same range of meanings as in standard French, be taken to mean an idea or concept of something, here, a concept or manifestation of the divine. Finally, John Kent (Kent 1987, 220) has pointed to the fact that western religious creativity does not work too well any longer with orthodox Christian symbols. He sees a death of religious images happening in western culture, worse than any previous death of religious images. While this possibility may be disconcerting to those who find themselves at home with such symbols and images, it should not prove a problem for an actual divine transcendence, since that divinity must still be capable of communication with the serious open-minded seeker after truth. When traditional symbols and images no longer appeal, there remains an infinite number of ways in which an actually transcendent God could communicate with people, e.g. through secular books, films, and paintings.

(e) Something about Prayer

Those who think that apparent manifestations of the divine must in some way be only subjective to humanity may therefore think the terms "God" and "the divine" do not stand for an objective reality. On such a view, a God or divinity cannot have personal communication with people, or people with God. Yet those who see God in terms of an impersonal, immanent, background to the world, or as a deistic God outside things, also have difficulties concerning communication between the divine and humans. This difficulty appears particularly when it comes to the subject of prayer. In addition to this are the difficulties that some report with prayer and contact with the divine from the human side of things, difficulties that cannot be swept aside by blaming each time the person doing the praying. Those who do not think there is a personal God who responds to prayer seem inclined to cite examples of people's prayer difficulties to support their attempt to reinterpret prayer in order to make it acceptable to people. In this section I will therefore briefly consider the topic of prayer difficulties before taking a look at some attempts to reinterpret or explain prayer in terms of something else.

Michael Goulder tells us that although he spent a lot of time each day in prayer, he found private prayer a barren exercise despite the fact that he read widely about methods of prayer and sought help from those with a reputation for holiness. He also found after thirty years in the Anglican ministry that reports made to him of religious experience and positive prayer experience were rare (Goulder & Hick 1983, 4-5, 27, 61-62). He finally concluded from this that God did not exist and resigned his pastorate. C.S. Lewis also experienced prayer difficulties as a boy, since he had been taught to say prayers and to think about what he was saying. This led him to critical philosophical analysis each prayer time as to whether he had been praying properly, and prayer time gradually became a burdensome nightmare. In Lewis' case, he came to understand that this approach to prayer was entirely false, and later in life he was to write about prayer, pointing out that many thought prayer meant merely to say prayers (Lewis 1977a, 53-55; Lewis 1977b, esp. 65-66). John Spong also describes his battles with prayer, and his attempts to deal with his experience of lack of contact with God by seeking help from numerous books on prayer (Spong 1999, 136-37).

A final example here comes from a young Anglican I once knew, who was given by his pastor at confirmation a little book on prayer. The book contained advice on morning and evening prayers, and instructed the young man in a prayer routine of adoration, thanksgiving, confession of sin, and intercession. There were prayers to be said at each of the prayer times, but in the book there was a list of topics to suggest what one might thank God for, and a list of topics to suggest what one might pray for. Like Lewis, the young man got himself into philosophical difficulties considering the lists, especially the intercession topic list, and gradually fell into despair concerning the list, since he felt that there was far too much in the world he should be praying for, and he did not know where to draw the line. Finally he threw out the book because he felt he could not cope with the burden of lengthy intercessions given that he had a full- time job and family commitments. Nor did he do better when he attempted to move on to books of meditations. Consulting those he deemed advanced in prayer did not help either, since he found himself directed to works by experts in mystical prayer such as Evelyn Underhill, Teresa of Avila and John of the Cross and found them totally unhelpful to his situation. Not surprisingly, the young man simply gave up.

Since I am not qualified to discuss particular cases and suggest why, on the view that there is an actual transcendent God, some believers have great difficulties with personal prayer, I will confine myself to two comments. First, that the situation may be the same for those praying as it is for those not having religious experiences. It may be that some people have experiences of God in prayer and others do not because they are constructed differently. This would not mean that God does not hear prayer, it would merely mean that a person did not have personal God experiences. Naturally one would have to ask whether there might also be factors at work such as self-centredness in prayer, careless recitation of set prayers, or even experimentation, as when Edmund Gosse as a boy tested his father's precepts on prayer by experimentally praying to a chair (Gosse 1986, 63-67; Lewis 1977a, 22-23). One might also question the rather dubious assumption that God or the divine ought to be manifest to the individual in prayer in some experiential manner. This rather suggests the possibility that a number of those with prayer difficulties might regard prayer as a failure because there was no divine manifestation or personal response. Yet this may be but a short step to seeking new forms of prayer in order to produce such a response. Finally, one cannot rule out that each individual needs to find his or her own method of prayer. I suspect that what often happens to believers is that it is decided for them early on how they should pray and they feel guilty when they find it burdensome. It is therefore not surprising that they end by stopping the prayer attempt in order to free themselves from stress and guilt. Thus one can sympathize with Michael Goulder and John Spong in their attempts to find a prayer method that worked, while asking about the criteria they were using to judge whether or not prayer "works," or whether one should think about prayer at all in that manner. A classic example of the attempt to analyse prayer is that undertaken by D.Z. Phillips. In his 1965 book, *The Concept of Prayer*, he concentrates on the feature of language, rejecting attempts by other philosophers to distinguish between belief in God and belief that God exists. For Phillips, philosophers who want to prove or disprove God's existence, thinking there is a reality test independent of language, are on the wrong track. Instead, one needs to examine the cultural context surrounding the concepts of God and prayer and ask what can and cannot be said about the concepts. The criteria of truth and falsity in religion are to be found within the religious traditions, but the criteria cannot say factually whether a religion is true or false. So the philosopher cannot answer the question of truth; the situation is one of examining meaning, not of verification. Phillips therefore aims to clarify the conceptual groundwork needed for an understanding of prayer. He wants to show what kind of activity prayer is, to say what people are doing when they pray (Phillips 1965, 8-13, see 23-29, 33, 38, 82-83, 91-93, 157-58). Whereas Phillips' approach is helpful to the extent that he makes a clear distinction between prayer and superstitious incantation, and (citing Simone Weil) between a "natural" God, to whom human ideas of power and self-assertion are ascribed, and a "supernatural" God embodying sacrificial love and self-denial (Phillips 1965, ch. 6, & 83, 98-102, 158-60; see Weil 1959, 101-02; Weil 1963, 10, 30), there are difficulties with his account of prayer.

First, Phillips stops with a discussion of the meaning of language. While he is correct to indicate the existence of the metaphysical barrier where proving or checking the reality of God's existence is concerned, there are problems with his attempt to set up God as a kind of eternal value or concept. This, it seems to me, occurs when he considers arguments by Anselm, Kant, and Norman Malcolm concerning God's necessary existence (Phillips 1965, 14-18). Phillips seems to conclude that since necessary, eternal existence is an intrinsic property of God in the Anselmian argument, then it makes no sense to argue as Kant does that one can deny the existence of an absolutely necessary being with all its predicated properties. Yet the statement "God is eternal and necessarily exists" is not the same kind of statement as "a bachelor is an unmarried man," where existential reference is concerned, even if it is seen as conceptually the same kind of statement. With the latter, we refer to a known, defined, specific personal status. With the former, we do not know that there is a divinity with its necessary/eternal predicates. We cannot scientifically check the state of affairs in the universe concerning God. Phillips and those agreeing with him seem ready to consider the God statement might be viewed as an existential one, having reference to existence, but they then ask what kind of existential statement it is. To what area of existence does it refer? Phillips sums up by pointing to the difficulty of comprehending the idea of an eternal God and says: "To have the idea of God is to know God" (Phillips 1965, 17-18).

Part of Phillips' argument for taking the proposition "God is eternal and necessarily exists," and similar expressions, as the working God statement for his book, seems to rest on the assumption that if one asserts the possible non-existence of this God one is falling for the error of seeing the God question as one about an existent something among other existent things. One is said to hanker after "the old spatial model" in which God's reality is likened to the existence of the planets, concerning which reality one can pose questions about the duration of the divine existence (Phillips 1965, 15-23, 41, 57-58, 81). To me, this suggestion seems to be cousin to the idea of God as an ancient, white-bearded old man, since to consider whether or not there is an eternal divine power behind the universe does not, as I have tried to show, entail that one must have a notion of God as an entity among other entities.

Second, Phillips in his book seems to presuppose that there is no actually transcendent God. Although he rightly indicates that philosophy cannot answer metaphysical questions of that kind, the assumption that there is no actually transcendent (or immanent) God drives the discussion of prayer throughout the book and unintentionally limits the description of it. Phillips stops with language in that he refers criteria of truth and falsity to the relevant religious contexts. God's eternal existence remains the basic value proposition that he works with. This enables him to avoid the metaphysical barrier so he can concentrate on the meaning of what people are doing when they talk to God (Phillips 1965, 23), although he cannot avoid contact with non-conceptual experience. Phillips says he does not deny that people feel presences or hear voices in religious experiences; he thinks science cannot exclude the possibility of miracles (which he defines as events that defy scientific explanation). He also mentions answered prayer, and he states that he does not deny prayer can have physical effects (Phillips 1965, 135-36, 119, 121, 144; see Keightley 1976, 67, 94, 99, 124, 126). Yet, every time Phillips turns the discussion to a question of meaning, his position indicates that such experiences could not be a product of his idea of the eternal God. Rather than stop neutrally at the metaphysical barrier, he explains prayer in terms of what seems to be his idea of the person's activity when that person is praying authentically. Prayer in his book seems always in fact to be addressed to God understood as a conceptual value or idea in order to enable the discussion to continue. Although believers in an actually transcendent God report their God relationship as one with a real, divine presence and not to a concept, Phillips thinks the idea of God, as a person capable of communication, suggests the attribute of finitude, and he uses comparisons with human situations to exclude actual transcendence (Phillips 1965, 43-52). His presupposition seems to be that God cannot be personal or communicate with humans except in a purely this-worldly setting where the word "God" appears to act as the necessary conceptual sounding board for avoiding the thought that the prayer is in fact directed only to empty air. Phillips also discusses the Paley-Hume arguments about a divine designer, concluding that nothing seems to count for or against a divine explanation of the world (Phillips 1965, 84-86, 95), though of course since 1965 the debate about design has become scientifically more sophisticated.

That prayer is understood as directed to what is a value (rather than to an existential reality that would meet Bernard Williams' criterion), does not manifest itself immediately when Phillips discusses forms of prayer, since it is easiest to make confession and thanksgiving accord with his God concept. Yet even here there are difficulties. Confession of sin is explained in terms of learning to know something about oneself one did not know before; it is also seen as confession of one's inadequacy. The problem here is that in confession one is primarily admitting to what one does know about oneself or previously did not want to admit, and the presupposition is that one can do better by striving to do better in future—a feature of confession that remains in the background in Phillips' account. Nor does Phillips seem to have place for the priest or pastor as the "mechanic" one can turn to for help. Prayers of worship and thanksgiving are viewed in terms of "religious" dependence on God, of living self-denyingly, and thanking God for our life as a whole irrespective of how life goes (Phillips 1965, 56, 59-60, 62, 68, & chs. 5 & 6).

Petitionary prayer is understood not as an attempt to influence the way things go but as an expression of, and request for, devotion to God through the way things go. Prayers for others are to be seen in terms of committal of the self trustingly to God, and one can want or pray that the person prayed for will view things in the same way. To pray for others does not need to entail ideas of telepathy, rather it is a matter of love in the hearts of the praying community; the thought of others praying for one can be a source of strength and power. Praying activity in community also testifies to the community's love of God and can influence others, causing them to turn to God. Phillips on petitionary prayer is puzzling, however, because, apart from any other problems with his account of prayer, he wants to retain the ambiguity of the idea of "love of God." He explains love towards God as a sort of emanation of God's love for people and entailing having God in one, but it is not clear what this can mean except as a kind of love of an idea or concept or love generated in community, especially when Phillips tries to keep psychological considerations out of the picture. With cases of God's talking to people, Phillips embeds such accounts in specific communities of understanding. For example, Hebrew prophets and Pentecostalists are viewed in the context of a tradition (Phillips 1965, 121-24, 127-28, & ch. 7, esp. 135-43, 127).

Where a miracle could be seen as the answer to a prayer, Phillips suggests that it is the community who decides whether the miracle event has a divine origin. Yet this again side-steps the issue of actual transcendence, and the matter is further confused when Phillips cites Lessing's famous essay "On the Proof of the Spirit and of Power" (Lessing 1957, 51-56) to show that the significance of many reported miracles is lost for us because we have lost the link between miracle and the living community in which it was performed. Yet Lessing is surely saying something somewhat different, namely, that it is one thing to witness a miracle and another to rely on a report of what one has not seen. He also makes the point, more relevant to Phillips' argument here, that the performance of miracles cannot be used to prove the truth of metaphysical statements made about the performer of miracles. All this, however, can hardly entail Phillips' conclusion from Lessing's arguments that it is the community that determines what is religiously significant (Phillips 1965, ch. 7, esp. 144-47).

To sum up here, what Phillips seems to have overlooked in his project is that he imprisons the entire discussion of prayer within a limited linguistic framework in which he presupposes that the idea of God as an absolute reality must be analysed philosophically in expressive and non-factual terms. He cannot, as a philosopher, presuppose the existence of an actually transcendent God, nor does he want to presuppose the opposite. This then leaves him with the concept of an eternal God as a value or idea to which the believer relates. At the same time, his application of philosophical logic, while fine for this-world situations, may turn out to be highly inappropriate with reference to reality in its entirety including the other side of the metaphysical barrier. We have already encountered situations that defy ordinary logic in the amazingly contradictory behaviour of particles. Hence to ask about the grammar of our idea of God (Phillips 1965, 82, 83) may be something that cannot be done with any satisfactory result where God is concerned, and also where prayer is concerned, since such an account cannot fail to be unintentionally reductive. In his criticism of the idea that prayer can necessitate what is prayed for, and that people misunderstood the thought that all things are possible for God, Phillips is bound to his idea of what is logically possible and to his God concept. He rightly points out that logical impossibility and God do not go together, but this does not mean that what we perceive as impossible is impossible for God, nor does it mean that it is thought prayer necessitates what is prayed for when a person prays, e.g. for the recovery of another person if God sees it as the right thing for that other person. Phillips is absolutely correct to draw our attention to the problem of what may seem to us to be unanswered prayer, but his solution is to conceptualize the entire issue in what inevitably has to be a limited framework.

A problem Phillips has overlooked in his project is that prayer is not a concept or something to be viewed from the outside, even though one can speak conceptually about religious matters. To take an analogy from daily life, a husband can believe his wife loves him and that he has a relationship with her. If, however, he begins to think about what it ought to mean that his wife loves him—whether she does in fact love him—even that he perhaps does not have a genuine relationship with her, then the husband has abstracted from the real relationship and is focussing on something that is likely to crumble away on analysis. His wife may well love him ardently, but since her love cannot be laid out in the scientist's laboratory and compared with the loves of other women for husbands, he has embarked on a fruitless task. It is only in the existential conversation and relationship that the husband can relate to his wife. If he concentrates on the language used in the relationship or on the concept of marriage, he is not likely to get very far. It is interesting to note here that John Polkinghorne emphasizes prayer as an interaction between individuals and God (Polkinghorne 1994, 62-78; see Polkinghorne 1989, 69-76).

John Spong devotes an entire chapter to "The Meaning of Prayer in a World with No External Deity" (Spong 1999, 134-48 esp. 135-36). He asks whether one can still pray "if there is no theistic deity who can respond personally to our prayers." What is most surprising about Spong's chapter is his expressed ardent wish to be "a person of prayer." He says he has longed for a sense of immediate contact with the divine, yet at the beginning of his book, as we noted earlier, he tells us that he lives in "a constant and almost mystical awareness of the divine presence" (Spong 1999, 3, 142-43, 146, 148).[19] Accepting that his second statement is correct, what are we to make of the first? Here setting aside, however, the problem of this apparent contradiction, we can follow him in this chapter from his reported unavailing struggles with prayer to his conclusion that the problem lay with the traditional God he had been taught to pray to. In his criticism of the Lord's Prayer, Spong's problem is not, as one might expect, that Jesus apparently suggested the saying of a prayer when the disciples asked him to teach them about prayer; his problem is with the fact that Jesus prayed to a heavenly father, and with several other features of the prayer. He thinks that Jesus suggested in the prayer that God enjoyed being flattered, and he lists terms such as "almighty" and "most merciful" as terms of flattery. He then defines prayer as the experience of meeting God, the intention to relate to life's depths, the offering of life and love in sharing friendship. It is also taking proper political action and facing the ups and downs of life.

The difficulty with Spong's approach here is that when he redefines prayer in this chapter (Spong 1999, ch. 9, esp. 136-39, 143, 147), the definitions get out of hand. One might well want to say that in one's prayer one meets God, if that happens to be one's experience, although such a statement suggested as a general definition creates problems for those who do not have a God experience when they pray. Yet to make "prayer" cover friendship, good political action, and facing the ups and downs of life, is to stretch the notion of prayer like a piece of elastic. One also wonders what humanists are to make of such a label, since one can hardly presuppose that humanists and atheists are incapable of loving friendships, proper political action, etc., but they would scarcely view themselves as praying. Finally, when he takes objective words such as "almighty" and "everlasting" to be terms of flattery, it seems to me he is guilty of taking a prayer response out of context. If a person's response to the divine power is one that naturally expresses itself in those terms, I fail to see why the praying person is guilty of flattery—unless that person is using such terms in an attempt to manipulate God in some way. I suspect here that Spong is reacting to prayers he was encouraged by his tradition to say, whether or not he felt them to be appropriate. Yet all this is not the same as the question of a person's God concept and ought not to be confused with it.

Nor is it very helpful when there is an attempt to redefine prayer on the basis of its effectivity in bringing about change in oneself. In the 1993 Richard Attenborough version of the film *Shadowlands*, about the life of C.S. Lewis, Lewis is made to declare that prayer does not change God, it changes him. D.Z. Phillips, quoting Kierkegaard, also makes the same observation (Phillips 1965, 56-57, 109; see Kierkegaard 1993, 22-23). Kierkegaard, however, is talking about an element of the confession of sin, not petitionary prayer, and one needs to be aware of shifts concerning the concept of change. God is not changed when people pray, and certainly not in the sense of dancing to the whims of a person praying self-centredly. A person may well be changed in the process of praying as one result of prayer, but such a statement acts as a subtle evasion of the question of prayer. It also implies that it is incorrect to view God as changed by prayer, as if this is what people praying authentically, that is, not self-centredly, think they are doing. In a relationship, however, someone responding to a situation is not changed, that person does something. What is done may be something that is manifestly a response, or it might be something indirect, so that someone making a request would not necessarily realize that there had been any response from that person to the situation. One might apply this analogy to God. God does not have to be changed in a divine response to a situation, even though God changes things in some way. Thus personal change, at least on its own, is not a very effective defence of prayer. It builds on a misunderstanding of the idea of change where God is concerned. Where the person is concerned, it could be argued that, if necessary, there are many other ways of bringing about change in oneself, such as consulting a psychiatrist.

Kierkegaard, as his pseudonym Johannes Climacus, also raised the question of what it meant to pray, and of difficulties connected with prayer (Kierkegaard 1992, 162-63, 177-79), yet his most insightful work on prayer is to be found in his discourses, not least in his *Upbuilding Discourses in Various Spirits* and in *Works of Love*. In the latter book, God is the "middle term" in relationships, but one is to love God above everything else (Kierkegaard 1993; Kierkegaard 1995, 44-60 esp. 57-58; see Matt. 22 v. 36-40). While Kierkegaard clearly does not think of God as external in the way an object is an entity external to one, his God is transcendent, and he is happy to talk of "heaven" in his writings (Kierkegaard 1967-78, II, F-K, entry 1502). Therefore what needs to be remembered is that when people have an idea of God as personal and transcendent, it does not mean that they are thinking of a Santa Claus figure in the sky. Nor does it mean they must have defective ideas about prayer, or that prayer does not "work" if one has a particular idea of God. It is thus not adequate to accuse defenders of theism of feeling threatened by, or frightened of, "modern" ideas about God, when they can be justifiably critical of what is presented them on the subject of God and prayer (Spong 1999, 68, 140, 226).

Chapter Three
About Miracles

In this chapter I wish to take a look at the topic of miracles, since their possibility is rejected not only by some in science, but also by some coming from religious traditions. For many in both religion and science, the claim made that miracles occur proves to be a stumbling block. Miracles are thus often regarded as old-fashioned religious baggage that needs discarding. In this chapter I will look at the definition of a miracle, then I will consider Hume's famous case against miracles, analysing some problems with his account. Finally I will consider miracles that appear to violate the laws of nature, with reference to some modern objections.

(a) The Definition of a Miracle

In the Danish dramatist and pastor Kaj Munk's play *The Word* [Ordet] (Munk 1963), the central theme is that of miracles. Munk explores the issue of the lack of miracles in his time (early to mid 20th century), and his conclusion is that it is because of lack of faith. The play in fact contains a dramatic miracle in the final scene and expresses Munk's feeling as a pastor that a Christian pastor with sufficient faith ought to be able to perform a miracle, just as Jesus did. Clearly Munk's observations on the subject are based on the assumption that we live in a universe where it is possible for miracles to occur under the correct subjective conditions (the faith of the individual or individuals). For Munk, there is nothing about the way things are objectively in the universe that makes miracles an impossibility. Yet for British philosopher David Hume (1711-1776) (Hume 1902, 109-31), miracles do not occur because of the nature of the objective world. Thus, at the outset, it is clear that if one thinks that the entire universe is in some way all of one piece or system, such that there can be no God or intervention from a God outside the system, then it is not possible to hold such a God responsible for amazing events that appear to defy the laws of physics. One must seek an explanation in relation to the ordinary laws of physics or at most in a revision of the laws (as was the case with the advent of Einstein's theory of relativity). If, however, one thinks the universe contains some eternal dimension beyond the scope of the natural order, then one may well think there could be some divine agency able to intervene in human affairs even if one does not attribute major natural catastrophes to interventions by that agency.

It is important, when examining the question whether the divine can or does intervene through the phenomenon of miracles, to clarify what a miracle is. Not infrequently, people speak of "the miracle of the human eye" or say that "each new-born baby is a miracle." Here, "miracle" is used as an expression of wonder at the astonishing complexity, beauty, etc. of nature. There is no suggestion at all that the human eye or the event of a new-born baby is unusual or somehow breaks the laws of nature. Indeed, part of the wonder lies in the fact that the laws and workings of nature are able to produce both. Thus the birth of babies and the various processes in nature, however wonderful they may be, do not constitute miracles. David Hume defines a miracle as "a transgression of a law of nature by a particular volition of the Deity, or by the interposition of some invisible agent" (Hume 1902, 109-31 esp. fn. 115). C.S. Lewis, who defended the possibility of miracles,[20] defines a miracle as "an interference with Nature by a supernatural power" saying of it that it "is emphatically not an event without a cause or without results. Its cause is the activity of God: its results follow according to Natural law. In the forward direction (i.e. during the time which follows its occurrence) it is interlocked with all Nature just like any other event. Its peculiarity is that it is not in any way interlocked backwards, interlocked with the previous history of Nature" (Lewis 1974, 9, 59-66 esp. 63-64). Both definitions thus contain the idea of interference with nature by a supernatural power. Unlike Lewis, however, Hume mentions two possible sources of the activity: God or an invisible agent. Unlike Hume, Lewis denies that a miracle is something that breaks the laws of nature.

Here, we need to consider what is meant by "the laws of nature." When we talk about the laws of physics or the laws of nature, it is clear that we are raising major issues. What are the mathematics that are used to describe the workings of the universe? Is mathematics a language, a tool made by humans for describing nature, or is it a universe in its own right? Peter Atkins (Atkins 1994, 99-125 esp. 109; see Barrow 1992) asks why mathematics works, and he makes the distinction between what he calls "strong deep structuralism" and "weak deep structuralism." By the former term, he means the view that the physical world has the same logical structure as mathematics, physical reality and mathematics therefore being identical, and by the latter, he means the view that mathematics and physical reality only share the same logical structure, so that one uses mathematics to mirror nature. Whatever we may conclude about mathematics and the nature of the laws of physics, it is clear that we need to take care not to assume that we know for certain the answer to the question and then conclude that miracles are impossible and that reports of them are erroneous in some way. Nor is it clear that any definition of mathematics would necessarily preclude the possibility of miracles.

C. S. Lewis in his book *Miracles* gives three definitions of "laws of nature." First, that we know from observation that nature behaves in a certain way, even if we do not know why, and the laws of nature are thus brute facts; second, that the laws of nature consist of applications of the law of averages, the actual foundations of nature being random and lawless; third, that the laws of physics are necessary and essential the way the truths of mathematics are. Lewis concludes that none of these definitions exclude the possibility of miracles, even on the view that the laws of nature are necessary, since God, in the case of a miracle, adds a new element to the situation, namely the exercise of supernatural force (Lewis 1974, 59-63). The point Lewis is making is that laws of nature do not themselves purposefully instigate events or actions. The events or actions are interpreted in the light of the laws bringing them about. It can also be added that attempts to define and describe the scope of mathematics and physics brush against the metaphysical barrier. We cannot step out of ourselves, our way of doing things, and out of the universe in order to get a clear answer to all our questions in this area.

(b) Hume's Essay "On Miracles"

Unlike C.S. Lewis, who was, of course, a committed Christian, Hume seems to have been agnostic or thinly theistic concerning the possibility of a divine power behind the universe (Barbour 1997, 44). Important here is the fact that he was an empiricist. Scientific theories and laws were to be understood as derived from observation and induction. Hence it is not surprising that Hume attempted to stay with this approach in his thought about miracles.

When we turn to his essay, we can see that Hume's main arguments are as follows: Because of the element of error in human experience, we should accept alleged facts to the extent that the evidence supports them. In cases such as the sun rising, we can be almost certain this will happen. In other cases we weigh up the evidence and decide in favour of where the heavier balance of probability lies. Reports of eye-witnesses to events are helpful as a basis of reasoning, given that people tend to be truthful and have moderately good memories. In weighing up such reports, our ultimate standard of judgement is based on experience and observation. Hume says reports of something considered as evidence should receive less weight to the extent of the unusualness of the fact in question. In the case of some extraordinary claim, there is a conflict between the reports and reality as we have experienced it, whereas in the case of some fairly ordinary or probable claim, reality as we have experienced it supports the weight of the reports. It can be that our experience has not been wide enough to include some particular aspect of reality (e.g. desert dwellers may never have seen snow). We can be almost certain the sun will rise because there has never been a report of it doing otherwise.—Hume, of course, was cautious about the idea of certainty, since he realized there was a "problem of induction" in relation to the future. However many times something has happened, this is no guarantee that there will be another instance following the same pattern. Yet in the case of the sun, Hume must have felt reasonably optimistic that no cosmological catastrophe would intervene suddenly to prevent its normal activity.

In the case of miracles, however, Hume argues as follows: A miracle is a violation of the laws of nature; a firm and unalterable experience has established the laws of nature. We have the weight of uniform experience of the workings of the laws of nature against the alleged event. Hume considers uniform experience amounts to proof, because the fact weighed against the miracle is this uniformity. To upset this, you need an opposing superior proof. But no reports of a miracle can be enough unless the denial of such reports would be even more miraculous than the miracle. Thus we need to consider some form of mistake or deception in the case of the alleged miracle.

Hume argues first, that throughout history there is no miraculous event that meets the test of the denial being "more miraculous" than the event, and no way of excluding the possibility of deceit or delusion. Second, humans have a psychological love of the miraculous and thus are ready to accept miracles. There are numerous cases of fraudulent "miracles." Third, stories of miracle and the supernatural come from primitive and ignorant nations. Reports of miracle decrease in proportion to increase in enlightenment and knowledge. Miracles do not happen in modern times. Finally, there is no report of miracles that is not opposed by an "infinite number" of witnesses, since the miracles in the various religions on which the religions depend [in those religions founded on miracle and miraculous event], contradict each other. So not all religions can be true. In the case of an enormous weight of reports of miracles (e.g. that of the healings at the tomb of the Abbé Paris in France, mentioned by Hume), it is enough, he thinks, to set against this that it is impossible that the events reported could have been miraculous. Credulity and delusion are the best explanation. It is also hard enough to get at the truth of even ordinary events. So no reports of miracles have ever been good enough to make them probable, let alone prove them, and, given our experience of natural laws, no report of a miracle ever could be strong enough to prove it.

Hume seems to allow that there could be natural violations of the laws of nature that could be adequately testified to, such as an account of a universal darkness for a week, but he seems to see this in terms of an event for which we should seek explanation of the cause (i.e. that it is really some natural and explicable aberration). Hume refuses to allow that reports that e.g. Elizabeth I died and rose from the dead could be true. It must be fraud. Even if one ascribes this to God's power, this will not do because we can know God only through nature. He thinks lies and untruths are more common concerning alleged miracles than with any other matter of fact.

As Douglas Odegard points out (Odegard 1982, 37-46 esp. 38) Hume's argument moves from the issue of improbability and weak historical testimony to the claim that no testimony to a miracle could ever be conclusive.—Miracles are simply impossible because the laws of nature have no room for miraculous exceptions. So Hume's approach to miracles can be summed up as follows:

> A miracle is a transgression of a natural law by divine or some invisible agency.
> The notion of miracle arises in the primitive human mind.
> The idea of miracle as violation of a law of nature is impossible:
> a. On grounds of the weight of empirical experience of the workings of the laws of nature contra historical testimony to miracles—no testimony is sufficient.
> b. The laws of nature have no room for miraculous exceptions, so no amount of evidence could be conclusive.

(c) Hume and the Violated Laws of Nature

Whereas Hume is quite right to be suspicious of reports of miracles, and that there have been cases of fraud, there are difficulties with his picture of the situation. As an empiricist, he surely should not view the laws of nature as something set in concrete. Whatever view one takes of the nature of such laws, from the human perspective it is humans doing the investigating, and there is always room for revisions to laws where this is found to be necessary. The idea of violated laws seems to proceed from the prescriptions of the courtroom rather than from the scientist's application of such laws as descriptive and their formulation on the basis of scientific experience. Yet when Hume says "a firm and unalterable experience" lies behind the formulation of the laws of nature, commonsense and the problem of induction dictate that there is no absolute inevitability. One can, for example, think of all kinds of end-of-world scenarios to do with comets, etc., crashing into the sun, that might put an untimely end to it. Hume gropes towards this thought himself when he speaks of reports of a darkened earth, where one would accept the overwhelming testimony and "look for causes."—In other words, one would revise the law in question to take in the violation, so that it would not be a violation any more. So while humans have uniform experience of the workings of the laws of nature, Hume himself admits that one cannot speak for tomorrow, and he indicates changes in nature that can affect the law in question (Hume 1972, 127-28). It is therefore strange that the tenor of Hume's essay, at least in parts, seems to point to an assumption that the uniform workings of things, formulated in terms of general rules, could not possibly work otherwise.

I think the root of the problem with Hume's essay lies in his failure to make a clear distinction between "laws of nature," meaning the actual uniform workings of things, and "laws of nature," as the formulations by scientists of how things work. The actual state of affairs in the universe is what it is, irrespective of how much we have uncovered. With laws developed about the workings of nature, we have at least initially to do with humanly constructed formulations based on available evidence, whether these are merely our constructions, or whether they are what we have discovered to be the case. Physics and chemistry, for example, are based on statistically arrived at laws and experiment, which further reinforces Hume's inductive argument rather than any idea of a fixed necessity of things. Helpful here is C.S. Lewis' insight, that laws of nature are applied to events and actions—they are not conscious instigators of action. If we take Hume's own example of the report of the universal darkness, there might be several possibilities where causation is concerned. The darkness might be some regular feature that occurred once every billion or so years through some natural agency. Or it might be a one-off aberration, never to occur again during the natural life of the sun. In either case, the rule that the sun shines somewhere on our planet every day would appear to be violated, even though the laws of nature were not in fact violated. To a certain extent, humans might be able to track down the cause and apply the relevant law responsible for the event, but one can envisage limit situations where the final explanation in a chain of events is missing because the metaphysical barrier is encountered. Therefore it might never be possible to explain why a particular event had occurred.

Because Hume seems to let himself be dazzled by the idea of violated laws, when he encounters an apparently well-attested instance of miracles, he opposes to the quantity of the reports his claim that it is impossible that they should have happened (Hume 1902, 124-25, 344-46). On the one hand he is prepared to accept the weight of evidence, as with his imagined universal darkness; on the other, we are to discount historical reports when they are not in favour of the case he wishes to make. Hume also exaggerates the case for gullible and primitive human nature wanting to accept miracles. Nor can Hume go from the situation in his day, when people tended to cite New Testament miracles as evidence for the truth of Christianity, to the loose assertion that religions generally are founded on competing miracles. Also, if there were few accounts of miracles in Hume's time, he is not entitled to conclude that this is because modern people are enlightened. As the work of Alister Hardy and David Hay and others (Heywood 1966, 26-31) has shown, large numbers of modern people both within and outside religions have reported personal religious experiences including seemingly miraculous events. The work of the Alister Hardy Institute in Oxford on reports of personal religious experience shows that people have tended to have such experiences and keep quiet about them for fear of being regarded as insane. Thus, the rise of science and the decrease of reports of miracle that Hume mentions is capable of a different interpretation. Nor are the ones having such experiences only the poor and illiterate. Large numbers of well-educated people in all walks of life appear in the research reports. Finally, Hume falls too easily for the myth of the primitive mind, where it is assumed that because a country is backward in science and technology, the people must inevitably have uncritical minds.

What is left out of Hume's account is the question of what or who instigates an event that looks like a violation of the laws of nature. If one holds the view that there is a God or divine agency responsible for the basic laws that activate the universe, and if one thinks that that God or divine agency can intervene in the world, it does not mean that a breach or violation of the laws of nature has occurred, any more than is the case with occasional natural catastrophic events. To give you an example of what I mean: Some summers ago I happened to see a small lizard by my back door. The lizard was on an area of concrete with the sun baking down on it, and it looked as if it were in distress. I was concerned that the heat might make it a problem for the lizard to make its way over a large (for a lizard) expanse of concrete to a shadier more friendly area of the yard. It managed to crawl feebly on to my rubber door mat, so I lifted the mat and moved the lizard to the shadier spot. Now from the lizard's point of view, something miraculous had occurred, since ordinary lizards (if they could be conscious of such things) know they cannot fly or be moved suddenly through the air in day-to-day life. Perhaps nothing like that happened to that lizard ever again. From my perspective, however, there was no miracle. It was merely my good will to the lizard that inspired me to move it to a better spot. If the lizard could have known how I had actually worked the move in terms of physics, it would not have thought of it as a violation of the laws of nature, but as an intervention. It would be understandable in terms of being an intervention by a higher agency.[21]

(d) Miracles and Modern Objections

We saw earlier that Rudolf Bultmann thought one could not believe in the "New Testament world of spirits and miracles" (Bultmann 1961, 5). Today the debate still continues, with voices in both religion and science accepting and rejecting the possibility that miracles can occur. Richard Swinburne, for example, defines miracle as "an event of an extraordinary kind, brought about by a god, and of religious significance" (Swinburne 1970, 1, 11, 13). For Richard Dawkins, what people call miracles he sees not as supernatural, but as "part of a spectrum of more-or-less improbable natural events." If a "miracle" occurs at all, it is "a tremendous stroke of luck" (Dawkins 1991, 139). Here, we need to bear in mind, after the previous discussion, how we are going to define miracles if we wish to avoid the idea of "violation" of laws. As a further working definition, we may want to revise Hume and say that a miracle is some kind of intervention, apparently by a divine power, that appears to violate the laws of nature. We also need to bear in mind that someone might regard as a miracle an event that appeared to be a divine intervention that did not seem to break any laws.—As an example of this I can mention a case reported to me in the 1990s by a first-hand witness, where an Australian family in an area of acute drought was in great need. For various reasons, their food supply had almost run out. A member of the family prayed to God for help, and very shortly an unknown person turned up with some food for them.—At this point, it is easy to get bogged down in endless discussion of whether a particular event fits the miracle category, and whether something that appears to be a miracle is an event that in fact has a perfectly natural explanation. It can also be debated how far such events are purely parapsychological, rather than religious in any way, and whether one can establish a borderline between something parapsychological and something spiritual. I would like to avoid this discussion, since it is dealt with in other places (Williams 1990; Grey 1993) and is, in my view, not really something that can be decided in the abstract. Every case of alleged miracle needs to be assessed with an open mind before deciding whether one is up against fraud, mistaken belief, or a genuine case of miracle.

For the sake of the discussion here, I will select one example of miracle type that appears to break the laws of physics as we know them. In the New Testament, Jesus is reported as having fed several thousand people with just a few loaves and fishes (Matt. 14 v. 15-21 & 15 v. 32-38; Mark 6 v. 34-44 & 8 v. 1-9, 19-20; Luke 9 v. 12-17; John 6 v. 1-13). There has been much debate about the New Testament miracles. Reginald H. Fuller (Fuller 1963, esp. 18-20) reminds us of this debate and discusses the question in detail in relation to text-critical issues. Those who have viewed some of the miracles as scientifically impossible have tried to find other solutions. For example, sceptics have suggested Jesus got the crowd to share their sandwiches or have urged that the story is a legend. Fuller points out that arguments about the genuineness of the miracles are irrelevant to the New Testament material, since the question of the New Testament miracles is an historical one, and all one can do is to lay aside preconceptions about miracles and study the traditions recorded in the gospels to see if it is possible to trace them back to Jesus himself.

It has to be agreed that it is difficult to deal with two thousand year-old miracle reports, and that Fuller's approach is the correct one where the New Testament is concerned. This is why I will also take another example of the multiplication of food from much nearer our own time. In 1829, Jean Vianney, the pastor of Ars in France, discovered that the granary belonging to the free school he had established had run out of grain except for a couple of handfuls. The harvest had been bad, and the pastor could not go back to previous donors because they had already given all they could afford for his good causes. He thus had 60 children in need of food. Vianney went to the granary with a relic of Francis Regis, placed the remaining grains on it, and then asked his parishioners to pray. A few hours later, when the granary door was opened, a flood of grain came pouring down the staircase because the granary was full to the roof. Four or five years later, they were in a similar situation. This time the pastor's helper was told to put her yeast into the tiny bit of flour that was left and close the kneading-trough. The next day, when the helper went to make bread, she felt the dough swelling, and the more water she put in, the more the dough increased until the trough was more than full, and the helper was able to bake ten large loaves. Jean Vianney is also credited with a similar incident concerning an empty wine cask and with the multiplication of pumpkin in a dish (Molyneux 1869, 103-07; Ghéon 1946, 79-83; Sheppard 1958, 78-79; Trouncer 1959, 142-44).

Here, we have an instance of what I will call a red-blooded miracle that appears to defy the laws of nature as we know them. What explanation could be given for it in our time? In the field of science, physicist Paul Davies, as we saw earlier, has concluded that there is a natural designer God behind the universe, making clear that he does not believe in God as a person "in any simple sense" (Davies 1992, 17, ch. 8, esp. 204, 220; Davies 1984, 208). Paul Davies' God is an intelligent manipulator within the laws of physics, limited by the universe and its laws, so that there is seemingly no place for a miracle-performing God, who, whatever he does, must work within the laws of physics (Wilkinson, 1993, 108, 111-12; Davies 1984, ch. 14, esp. 198; Polkinghorne 1988, 55-56). Davies thinks that if the difficulties of establishing that such phenomena occur can be overcome, most people are going to refer them to the realm of parapsychology and mind-power, rather than ascribing the phenomena to God. Whereas Davies might be able to accommodate healing miracles within the laws of physics in parapsychological terms, it is hard to see how his view could accommodate red-blooded miracles that appear to break the laws of physics. It seems to me that if he accepts the authenticity of the accounts, he must postulate some radical revisions to the laws of physics in order to bring the miracle event within the scope of his view. If he accepted that the miracle was in some way linked to his designer God, this might prove very difficult, since he would be hitting the metaphysical barrier concerning how God must be situated in relation to the universe. He would need to show how his God related to the universe and was able to disturb our ordinary view of the laws of nature through such a miracle.

Physicist John Polkinghorne thinks that the future is open, allowing the divine power and humans to play parts in bringing it about. For Polkinghorne, a red-blooded miracle can be seen as unexpected and extraordinary, but like Davies, he does not want to see it in terms of interference with nature. Polkinghorne analyses types of miracle, viewing the healing miracles of Jesus as not contrary to the laws of physics because healing powers do seem to be possessed by some people, and he thinks they could be interpreted naturally, however amazing the results brought about by the healer. Polkinghorne thinks that other types of miracle, such as the account of Jesus stilling the storm, could rest on meaningful coincidences. Finally, however, there are miracles such as Jesus' changing of water into wine at Cana. To the question whether such miracles really happened or not, Polkinghorne's answer is that the question of miracles is a theological rather than a scientific issue. Science tells us that such events are against normal expectation, but it cannot exclude the possibility that God does do extraordinary things. Thus one need not hold the view that natural laws are violated. Polkinghorne thinks that there must, however, be some deep underlying consistency in the nature of God to make sense of such activity, since he would not be capricious (Polkinghorne 1994, ch. 6; Polkinghorne 1989, ch. 4, esp. 50). Like Davies, Polkinghorne seems to find the issue of red-blooded miracles tricky. His view would seem to accommodate non-red-blooded miracles fairly easily, but more would need to be said about God and the laws of physics to accommodate such red-blooded miracles as John Vianney's. One would surely have to posit different sets of laws of physics instigated by God, and assume that what we know is only one set, before we could easily keep the red-blooded miracle within laws of physics. We might have to posit laws of physics belonging to nature and another set belonging to supernature, but then we would be deeply into metaphysical assumptions.

Lurking behind this issue therefore is also the question of what "dualism" might mean concerning God and the universe. Because of Descartes, we perhaps too readily assume that the idea of dualism with respect to God and the universe must present the same interaction difficulties as Descartes' sharp distinction between mind and body. Yet is this necessarily the case? One can think of dualities where the two parts are totally different things, but one can also think of dualities where there is connected separation between two things, for example, the two rails of a railway track. Similarly, we need to have a clear understanding of how we are using the term "monism" in "dual-aspect monism," since the term can stand for a purely one-stuff view, or it can be loosely used to indicate that ultimately things in the universe are unified. Assuming that Polkinghorne is using the term in this latter sense, it is not clear that we are further forward, since "unity" again can suggest close connection, or it may be used to indicate that things are connected. In the latter case, we will need to know what things, and in what way.

Theologian John Hick considers various definitions of miracle. He describes a miracle, when it is viewed as a mixed scientific and religious concept, as seen as incapable of natural explanation, an event that could not have happened unless God had intervened in the workings of the universe to bring it about. Hick is dubious about this traditional view of miracles on the grounds of God's consistency. Hick wants to know why God does not intervene more often, especially when people pray about problems. Hick believes that it is better to think that God has respect for our freedom and responsibility and does not miraculously intervene in the sense of divine suspensions of natural law. Hick is not, however, saying that all reports of events regarded as miracles are to be dismissed. He points out the universe is a partially open system within which the freedom of mental life can interact with matter and affect what happens. Hick speaks of the mystery of the nature of mind and its activity, and says we can speak only in very general terms about "the system of mental and psycho-physical law" that permits miracles and other extraordinary events to occur. Here, Hick appeals to parapsychology and takes as his example amazing healings so that when they occur suddenly (Goulder & Hick 1983, 68-74, 40-41, 75, 78, 97, 106) or speedily, it suggests divine intervention. He refers the matter of healing, whether normally, or apparently miraculously, to the activity of co-operating with "God's prevenient activity." Hick thinks that we need a theology in which the entire process of the universe is seen as the divine creative action. He sees the divine purpose unfolding through evolution so that humans eventually become aware of their God-given potentialities. To be conscious of God is to be conscious of being part of the divine creativity and loved by God. By this, Hick does not mean that there is no contact between the divine and the human. Indeed, he gives personal instances of religious experience that indicate such contact. Yet it is clear that Hick finds it hard to accommodate miracles of the red-blooded variety.

(e) Epilogue
On the Status of the Divine Miracle-Worker

Against the idea of divine intervention John Hick gives the case of a plane journey he took across the Atlantic to London. Hick needed to arrive on time because of various arrangements in London, but the plane took off three hours late. Hick says that had he prayed to God about this matter, then he later might have thought his prayer answered, since the strength of the winds was such that the plane was able to land on time. Hick suggests even if he had made such a prayer, he would have been forgetting that the beneficial winds must have been retarding flights in the other direction and thus inconveniencing others (Goulder & Hick 1983, 78). Here, I think that a couple of things need to be taken into consideration. On the one hand, how urgent was it for anyone on Hick's plane to arrive on time? Hick cannot rule out the possibility that someone on the plane needed urgently to arrive on time for a very valid reason and did pray. If that had happened, the other part of Hick's problem, namely, that passengers in the other direction might have been inconvenienced, need not be a problem as long as Hick does not presuppose that God's mental powers are on a par with his own or any other human's. In other words, one can imagine a divine power able to straighten out the kinks, so that delay in the other direction did not cause an urgent problem for anyone.

I thus do not find Hick's example at all persuasive if it is meant to support the view that God never performs red-blooded miracles.

I find important, however, his rejection of an arbitrary God, and Polkinghorne's suggestion that if God performs a miracle, it must be in accord with an underlying consistency. There is a difference between e.g. wanting to arrive on time otherwise one might be late for a meeting, and a desire to arrive on time because it is a matter of life and death for someone. I also do not think it helps to ask why God does not perform miracles more often, since the answer to such questions lies on the other side of the metaphysical barrier. It seems to me that one cannot start from the theology. One must start from human experience, and not merely from instances when miracles and religious experiences do not occur. Red-blooded miracles do happen, and anyone who has witnessed one will know that it looks as if there has been intervention in the ordinary laws of nature. Having said this, it must remain a matter of investigation and faith how one regards a miracle of that kind. It is relatively easy to explain healings and sudden answers to prayer in terms of parapsychological influence. It is impossible to explain scientifically a red-blooded miracle if one has witnessed one. Such an event is as shocking as quantum theory (Davies 1984, 100).— In the final dramatic scene of his play *The Word* Kaj Munk creates this sense of shock by having a red-blooded miracle occur (the resurrection of a dead woman). While two of the witnesses (from different traditions in the Danish Church) accept the evidence of their eyes, the pastor denies what he sees, declaring it to be physically impossible. The doctor accepts what he sees, but opts for the theory that, despite the death certificate, the woman must have been only in some kind of a coma.

Here, I have to admit to a personal interest in the subject, in that many years ago in the 1960s, I was myself a witness to an event that fits the category of red-blooded miracle. The matter turned on a negative report written by a teacher for a person (whom I will call Jonathan, as it would be improper to reveal personal details) who was seeking admission to college. The report was written in all honesty by the teacher, whose information was based solely on impressions gathered from having taught Jonathan at school. The report had to be written on the reverse side of an application form and sent to the college. I got to hear that before Jonathan was due for an interview at the college, he went to see the teacher, who had already sent off the report in order to meet the application deadline. (Jonathan had been unable to visit the teacher earlier and had therefore sent the form to her). The teacher became convinced that the report (which had been very negative) did not reflect the current status of Jonathan, but she felt that it was up to him to argue the case with the college. Jonathan went rather nervously to the interview, and I went too as friendly moral support. The member of staff dealing with applications commented, however, on the lack of a report from the teacher, and even as Jonathan was explaining that a report had been sent, he took the application form out of the file and showed that the reverse side was blank apart from the printed rubrics. I happened to have been present when Jonathan sent off the form to the teacher, and we both recognized it as the one (the only one) he had put in the envelope and sent to his teacher. Initially one could assume that somehow the teacher had accidentally filled in something else and sent off the blank report to the college, although the teacher was known for paying careful attention to details. When questioned later, the teacher, who was absolutely baffled, was unable to explain what might have happened. She remembered filling in a form and mailing the form, but there was no trace of any other form on her desk with her report on it, nor did Jonathan ever get to hear that she had found one. Jonathan got his place in college, because, in the absence of a written report, the applications staff member rang the teacher to discuss the application and she now gave a positive recommendation.[22]

I put the incident in the red-blooded miracle box because it looked as if the laws of nature had been broken. I was even more bowled over by the incident when Jonathan told me that at the time when the blank form had been shown us, he had heard God's "voice" letting him understand that God was responsible for the removal of the negative report. Now Jonathan was not especially religious; he didn't have a history of mental illness. In my view he was a perfectly ordinary young man, just like any other young man wanting to go to college. On the theory that it was a red-blooded miracle, I do not think God broke any laws. Either God wiped the report off the form applying a rule of physics from a wider set of laws beyond our knowledge, or it might have been something simpler: that God provoked a situation in which the teacher somehow must have filled in another form by accident and this other form got caught up with other papers and thrown away.—Though here, however, I find the principle known as Occam's razor (that all things being equal one should go for the simplest explanation) unhelpful. The principle is fine for some situations, but in this case, it is hard to find any kind of genuinely simple explanation that is totally plausible given all the factors of the situation known to me.—Certainly, even setting aside Jonathan's report of the "voice," it could not be the case that the event occurred through parapsychology because people were praying for him, since no one else was aware of his situation or even that he was going for an interview. Thus, if one is going to invoke the possibility of parapsychological interference, the interference was certainly not done by the living, though Jonathan himself may have been praying. The important outcome of the situation was that Jonathan was rescued from unemployment punctuated by short bursts of rather meaningless employment and received a training that enabled him later to become a useful member of the community. Also, although he had previously been basically a happy person, he became even happier and more out-going than before.

I also have to add to this that, like John Hick, I have very occasionally had experiences of a religious (Goulder & Hick 1983, 40-41, 75) and of a parapsychological, nature. Like Rosalind Heywood (Heywood 1966, 26-31), I found the cultural climate somewhat hostile to such experiences, and also one feels disinclined to report experiences of a religious nature because they are too precious to be bandied about. What I will say here, however, is that such experiences are self-authenticating as they happen, just as one is in no doubt that one is in e.g. a car crash when it happens. It is also clear to me that the explanation that all such experiences are purely subjective productions or "hallucinations" will not do. I have also had the opportunity of hallucinating once or twice (once because of a fever and once because of the effects of an anaesthetic and pain-killing tablets), and the experiences are just not in the same category. In the light of the above, I think that we must regard the notion of "laws of physics" and "laws of nature" as being much wider than our present conception. At the same time, one needs to be critical where reports of miracles and mysterious happenings are concerned. Just as shop goods are subject to analysis and control to make sure that they are the genuine articles, so, too, we need to maintain a critical vigilance in relation to our own or anyone else's report of such experiences. This is the only way to maintain a safe-guard against self-deception and fraud. A divine power as source of truth must surely prefer such a stance to one of naïve gullibility.

Chapter Four
The Darwinian Red Herring

In this final chapter I would like to consider the issue of God and creation, since the debate surrounding Charles Darwin's theory of evolution has led a number of people to think that certain statements in the Bible about God and creation must be invalidated by Darwinism, and that therefore the Bible can have nothing to say to modern people. There are, of course, also those who think that Darwin's theory of evolution anyway automatically rules out the possibility of God's existence. I will therefore first consider statements made in the book of Genesis and Darwin's theory of evolution. Then I will take a critical look at neo-Darwinism, followed by a consideration of evolution as a concept. Finally, I will seek to show that the theory of evolution can never present a genuine problem for the believer in a divine power behind the universe.

(a) Creation Accounts in the Book of Genesis

I need to begin with a slight digression on the topic of truth. Especially with the advent of information technology, it is easy to get into the habit of seeing truth as something rather literal, and understanding statements, when they are not fictional, as either true or not true in a literal sense. An extreme example of this view comes, however, from the 19th century in the story of young Edmund Gosse, whose parents, especially his mother, kept fiction away from the boy on the grounds that it was not true (Gosse 1986, 48-50). Yet one can see another view of truth emerging in the 1993 film *The Shawshank Redemption*, where an innocent man is imprisoned for the murder of his wife. Initially, he protests his innocence, much to the amusement of the other prisoners, but he later sees himself guilty of killing her, not because he had anything to do with her death, but because, in the years of their marriage, he was unable to show his feelings to his wife, and this brought about the estrangement that drove her to taking a lover. When his wife is killed with her lover in the lover's house by a burglar, he happens to be close by in his car meditating a confrontation with the lover. He is drunk and has a gun; he broods over his domestic situation until he gives up the idea of confrontation and drives away. Yet he comes to see himself as having brought about her death because his closed up nature drove her away from him. Thus he has moved from a literal understanding of truth to another conception of the situation. He saw himself as having killed her psychologically, and of course the quarrel that caused her to go to her lover's house that night led to her physical death. We therefore need to think very carefully about the nature of truth, what it is, and how it is mediated to us. As any good philosophy dictionary will make clear, it is not easy to say what truth is, since there are several theories—for example, the correspondence and coherence theories of truth, to name but two. Having said this, we can now consider the account of creation in the Bible.

Not everyone is aware that there are, in fact, two accounts of creation at the beginning of the book of Genesis, the author of the book using them to provide a total account of creation.[23] In the first account, God creates the world in six days, starting with a dark, water-covered earth. He creates day and night; he separates the waters above the sky from the waters of the earth; he creates land and plant-life; then he creates the sun and moon, followed by the creation of fish and birds. Finally, he creates animals, then male and female humans to rule everything. On the seventh day, God can take a rest, because creation is now finished. Creation is shown as good, and plants and creatures are encouraged to procreate. In the second account, God starts with the situation of bare earth. Water wells up from the ground. Then God creates a man out of the earth dust, followed by creation of a garden with a river and two trees, a tree of life and a tree of the knowledge of good and evil. The man has to look after the garden and name the animals, and he is forbidden to eat fruit from the tree of the knowledge of good and evil. God then creates a woman from the man's rib. An evil talking snake tempts first the woman and then, through the woman, the man to eat the forbidden fruit. After they have done so, the pair become self-conscious and make leaf clothes. The result of their sin is expulsion from the garden with future tough work conditions, and death at the end of it. The man (Adam) and the woman (Eve) have two children.

The one son, Cain, murders his brother Abel and becomes a fugitive, settling down and marrying in foreign parts. Then Adam and Eve have another son, and we are given some details about the descendants of Adam and Eve's children. The account ends with people beginning to invoke God by name.

Now apparently, we have two rather different accounts, one in which God starts with a rather dark and watery situation, and another in which he starts with a dry situation and an initial creation of a specific pair of people, with whom he talks in the garden. Certainly, if we take both stories to be literally true, we have problems, since there are discrepancies between them, and of course we want to know who was around to report what God was doing. If it is claimed that (unlike Islam, which says the Koran was divinely dictated to Mohammed) God inspired the human pen of the writers of the creation narratives, then we will also want to know why there is no mention of the inspiration event, no account of the divine contact with the human mediator, as there is, for example, with Moses and the Judaic law and with Mohammed and the Koran (Armstrong 1993, 31, 160-63). Also, if we look at other religious traditions, we will find that they, too, have accounts of creation, and that they are different from those in the Bible (Ballou 1948, 30, 165-68; Stewart 1989). Despite these difficulties, there are, as we will see, those who defend the literal truth of the combined account of creation, pitting it against Darwinistic evolution theory with its different account of biological origins over millions of years.[24] While I will not in this chapter be going into a discussion of the ongoing battle between Darwinism and creationism (the view that in its more extreme versions tries to provide a scientific basis for the literal truth of the Genesis creation account), those interested in the details of the biological, geological, and theological issues should read what the various creationist views have to say, in order to make an informed decision about them. There is a mass of material both for and against creationism (Brooke 1991, 343-45; Gish 1978; Denton 1985).

What does need addressing here is the assumption that all those for whom the Bible is their religious source book must inevitably take a literal view of all the biblical material, and especially that they must believe that the combined creation account of Genesis is literally true. John Spong tends to give one this impression when he speaks of the need for the Church to cease proclaiming that somehow the truth respecting God is still bound by our "literal scriptures or our literal creeds." Indeed, he goes even further and states that "for most of Christian history" this "myth" from Genesis has been treated literally (Spong 1999, 21, 86). Yet Spong must know that his assertion is extremely simplistic and misleading. As physicist Russell Stannard points out, in the early Church there were two schools of thought concerning the reading of Genesis. One school tended to be literalistic, the other treated the stories to a large extent as allegory. The Christian theologian Origen (ca. 185-254) did not treat Genesis as if it were literally true, and Augustine of Hippo, writing 1,400 years prior to Darwin's theory of evolution, said that at the beginning of things there were created only germs or causes of the forms of life which were to be developed gradually afterwards. The emphasis on a strictly literal approach to the Genesis texts occurred first with the advent of the Reformation in the 16th century (Stannard 1993, 17-24 esp. 21-22). To be fair to Spong, when he says the Genesis myth has been treated literally for most of Christian history, he is thinking at that point specifically of the second Genesis account with Adam and Eve. Yet he does not make any distinction between how the two accounts have been regarded in the Christian tradition, so the reader is left to assume Spong's statement definitely covers both creation narratives.

Nor does it help matters if we look only at the time when Darwin first produced his theory of evolution, since, as Robert M. Young points out (Young 1970, 13-35), just as is the case today, there were scholars with a foot in the camp of science as well as religion, and supporters of evolution theory simply cannot be treated as if they all rejected religion. On the contrary, efforts were made by evolutionists to reconcile religion and science as complementary pictures of the world, although attempts were also made, despite the difficulty of doing so, to keep science and theology separate in an analysis of scientific issues. Young shows that reactions to Darwin's theory at the time were highly complex. Literal interpretations of the Bible set against evolution theory came from those who were ill-informed about the theory, whereas the intelligentsia attempted to accommodate evolution theory to a natural theology. An unhappy attempt to unite evolution theory

with biblical literalism occurred, however, in the case of zoologist
and Plymouth Brother Philip Gosse (Gosse 1986, 101-06, 112-13,
149). Gosse experienced agonies concerning Darwin's evolution theory, which appealed to his scientific sense but went against his literal
understanding of the Genesis narratives. He attempted to reconcile
Genesis and science in his theory that when God created the world,
it immediately presented the appearance of a planet on which life had
existed for a very long time (Gosse 1857), and he was dismayed when
no one took his reconciliation seriously. The question at the time was
thus not whether or not there was a creator God, but the nature of
that God with respect to how that God governed things. Zoologist and
geologist Louis Agassiz (1807-1873) was unhappy with Darwin's theory
because he saw the idea of a divine mind behind creation threatened
by the alleged role of chance in natural selection (Brooke 1991, 47,
282-83). The evolutionists wanted a bigger picture of the creator, one
that emphasized God's government of the world through natural laws,
even though this made God more remote from the world. Charles
Babbage, father of the computer, attempted to show that apparent
miracles were instances of higher laws. For Darwin himself (whose
degree was in fact in theology) it was derogatory to the creator to
assume that he directly created parasites and worms rather than that
these creations came about through laws God instigated. Therefore,
despite the emphasis of the time on interpreting nature according to
fixed laws, and while all nature (including the human mind) could
be seen as subject to such laws, the whole of nature was viewed as
coming within the scope of God's law. The theory of evolution was
thus not seen by educated scholars and scientists as conflicting with
religious revelation. So even in the 19th century it is not possible to
make evolution theory stand for enlightened science minus God or a
divine power (Young 1992, 24-25), and it is noteworthy that when
Karl Marx wanted to dedicate the English edition of *Das Kapital* to
Darwin, the latter declined, because he did not wish to be associated
with attacks on Christianity and theism.

So great care needs to be taken not to ascribe a literal understanding
of Genesis to everyone in the Christian tradition. This does not mean
that the texts do not communicate truths. Russell Stannard sees among
the truths asserted by Genesis the following: that there is one creator

God, creator of everything. That God is personally concerned with all humans. We fall short of our God-given created potential and do wrong actions. The union of men and women is something sacred, and we are placed in the world to take care of it. John Polkinghorne understands the Genesis creation narratives as showing that the world and its process is a continual expression of God's creative will (Stannard 1993, 23; Polkinghorne 1988, 54). There can thus be differing perspectives on what truths are conveyed to the believer by the Genesis narratives, and there is no reason to find them a problem in relation to evolution theory. It of course still has to be remembered that the assumption that God exists and is a creator God is a metaphysical assumption to be accepted on the basis of belief.

(b) Darwin's Theory of Evolution

Turning now to Charles Darwin's theory of evolution, we need to consider some of the assumptions made by him, and whether the theory by itself (i.e., not viewed in relation to the Book of Genesis) could provide any hindrance to the possibility of an actually transcendent God. Darwin started his career path attempting to train as a doctor like his father, but when this did not work out, he was sent to read theology at Cambridge, where he developed a serious interest in botany. After his voyage on the *Beagle* in 1831 as ship's naturalist, Darwin began to make a name for himself as a geologist. He was to spend the rest of his life doing the biological research that in 1859 led to the publication of his theory of evolution (White & Gribbin 1995).

It has been said of Darwin that he became an atheist because of his discoveries, but his situation is more complicated than this. In his early twenties he lost faith in the literal truth of the Bible and its miracles, but he believed in Deism. Darwin's God was the unmoved mover, and he was much influenced by the work of William Paley (1743-1805), who had put forward an argument from design for the existence of God. Paley had argued that just as a watch implied the existence of a watchmaker, so the world implied the existence of a creator, namely God. Darwin retained this view until the period of the beginning of *Origin of Species*, after which, influenced by Thomas Henry Huxley's way of thinking,[25] he came to be agnostic, though he was not comfortable with it (Ruse 1993, 249; White & Gribbin

1995, 224).—White and Gribbin think that Darwin moved on from agnosticism to atheism and then to an existentialist position. Ronald Clark (Clark 1984, 57-58) shows Darwin's situation as loss of religious belief partly because of his scientific findings, but partly because he found some Christian doctrines, such as eternal damnation, totally unacceptable. In public writings, Darwin was careful what he wrote about religious matters. My own view is that he might still have been agnostic about the possibility of a creator God, even though he rejected, as he did, Christianity along with the possibility of life after death.

Darwin's research leading to evolution theory began already from the time of the *Beagle* voyage, and it is said that he was influenced by Charles Lyell's geological studies and Thomas Malthus' work on population. Lyell in his *Principles of Geology* (1830-1833) supported the uniformity of the laws of nature against the idea of divine catastrophic interventions (such as God's flooding of the earth reported in Genesis chs. 6-9), but he was unhappy with evolution theory to the extent he saw the theory threatening the idea of the uniqueness of the human species and as an explanation for the advent of the human mind. Malthus had written his *Essay on the Principle of Population* in 1798 (revised 1803), in which he argued for population control because he thought his calculations demonstrated that population increase would always outstrip the food supply. John Hedley Brooke (Brooke 1991, 248-54, 261) points out, however, that it is difficult to say with certainty which specific influences affected Darwin as he did his research. Darwin was reluctant to publish his controversial theory of evolution until he felt absolutely sure of his facts; he must also have been aware of the uproar it was likely to provoke from the general public.[26] When, in June 1858, after twenty years' research, Darwin discovered that Alfred Russel Wallace (1823-1913) had arrived at a similar theory of evolution, he was persuaded to join Wallace with a joint announcement of the theory and presentation of both versions at a meeting in London. In the spring of 1859, Darwin published *The Origin of Species*.

Darwin's observations of fossil remains indicated to him that species that used to exist no longer did so, and that there were new species that had not existed in the past. He also observed similarities between the anatomical structures of different species and was struck by the variations in individual species. At the end of his introduction to the first edition of *The Origin of Species* he says: "I am fully convinced that species are not immutable [unchangeable], but that those belonging to what are called the same genera are lineal descendants of some other and generally extinct species.... Furthermore, I am convinced that Natural Selection has been the most important, but not the exclusive, means of modification" (Darwin 1998, 7). Here, it is important to note the difference between two parts of Darwin's theory: evolution and natural selection. The word "evolution" in one sense can mean any process or formation or growth of something. Evolution in this sense is just "development." Evolution in a Darwinian sense, however, is a technical term indicating the continuous generic adaptation of organisms or species to the environment, this occurring through the integrating agencies of selection, hybridization, inbreeding, and mutation. It was this definition, containing the idea of natural selection, that singled out Darwin's theory from previous thought about evolution.—With the first sense of the term "evolution," a believer accepting the truth of the creation accounts in Genesis fairly literally might easily accept that the world had developed according to the laws of nature, treating each "day" of creation as covering huge spans of time (2 Pet. 3 v. 8). The fly in the ointment appears with the second definition of "evolution" with its notion of natural selection.

In Darwin's *The Origin of Species*, he thus presents a detailed case for his theory of natural selection based on the struggle for existence. He says: "I have called this principle, by which each slight variation, if useful, is preserved, by the term Natural Selection, in order to mark its relation to man's power of selection. But the expression often used by Mr. Herbert Spencer of the Survival of the Fittest is more accurate, and is sometimes equally convenient" (Darwin [1936], 52; see Young 1992, 160-61, 120-21, 132). Darwin was, however, a very open-minded and meticulous researcher. Therefore he also looked at some difficulties presented by the theory and considered objections brought against it (Darwin 1998, chs. VI-VIII; Darwin [1936], chs. VI-VIII). In 1871, he wrote a sort of sequel to *The Origin of Species*, namely *The Descent of Man*. In this sequel he begins with evidence for the descent of man from some lower form. He also discusses the manner of human development from a lower form, saying that: "some of the most distinctive characters of man have in all probability been acquired, either directly, or more commonly indirectly, through natural selection" (Darwin [1936], 441).

So on this theory, the characteristics of living things change, and a species can give rise to other species over a period of time. Overproduction of offspring leads to a struggle for existence in relation to the food sources, the fittest (those best able to evade predators and get at food) survive. Variations are inherited, so the traits that make for fitness continue. Darwin, having gone through objections that could be made to his theory, found nothing that could prove fatal to it, though he was to find the question of the age of the earth an extremely difficult problem. In 1871, biologist St. George Jackson Mivart, who was also a Roman Catholic, published a book *On the Genesis of Species*. While Mivart was open to Darwin's ideas in *The Origin of Species*, he drew the line at human evolution, at least where the human soul was concerned, and attacked the theory of natural selection. Specifically, he attacked the shortness of time available for evolution to do its work. Darwin had faced this criticism also from astronomers and physicists who were sure the earth could not be old enough to provide an adequate time-scale for the working of evolution by natural selection (White & Gribbin 1995, 250-56). So already in *The Descent of Man* Darwin, in the light of scientific objections, backtracked on the theory of natural selection: "I perhaps attributed too much to the action of natural selection or the survival of the fittest. I have altered the fifth edition of the 'Origin' so as to confine my remarks to adaptive changes of structure....if I have erred in giving to natural selection great power, which I am far from admitting, or in having exaggerated its power, which is in itself probable, I have at least, as I hope, done good service in aiding to overthrow the dogma of separate creations." (Darwin [1936], 441-42). By the 1880s this part of evolution theory had almost vanished.

In all this, is there anything in Darwin's theory of evolution by natural selection that attacks the idea that there could be an actually transcendent God? I think the reply to this depends on how one views the theory. As many have done, it is perfectly possible to presuppose on the basis of religious faith that there is an actually transcendent God and hold the theory of evolution to be true. In Darwin's time, as we have seen, the response of reputable scientists was to emphasize a deistic God; hence the idea of an actually transcendent God was pressed to the point of ultra-remoteness from the world. There was no question of e.g., identifying the deity in some way with the workings of the universe. If, however, one's religious belief rested on Paley's argument from design (Paley 1836, 387-487 esp. 393-96), then the situation is a bit different. Paley's argument, as we saw, rested on the analogy between a watch and a watch-maker. Since the world appeared to manifest design to an extraordinary extent, then one could ascribe the workings of the world "watch" to the divine watch-maker. Unfortunately it is not clear that the universe can be treated like a watch-like mechanism, or that the analogy is appropriate. At best, the argument can point a person in the direction of thinking about the amazing order of the world and whether there might be a divine power behind things. Paley went even further, in that he saw e.g. the human eye as divinely designed for the purpose of vision; so every feature of the world could be regarded as similarly planned for its task—every part of every organism had been designed for its function. With, however, the advent of Darwin's theory of evolution by natural selection, a rival explanation of the natural world arrived on the scene, in which eyes, ears, etc., occurred through natural processes. So, if one still wished to posit a divine creator behind the scenes, that creator acted indirectly through the laws of nature. On the other hand one could just as well posit that there were only the laws of nature and that there was no creator behind things.

On the scientific side of things, Darwin's theory seemed to be in a more precarious situation with respect to his contemporaries, since there seemed to be no scientific evidence that could show that the earth was more than a few thousand years old (Brooke 1991, 285). Yet his theory needed vast amounts of time. The state of science in Darwin's time, however, indicated that there simply could not be adequate time for the workings of the evolutionary process as Darwin presented it. The theory of evolution by natural selection needed a new physics, supporting a great age for the earth and sun, for it to be taken seriously.

(c) Modern Evolution Theory

Given that the science of our time seems to indicate that the sun and earth have endured for an enormous number of years, thus providing enough time for the evolutionary process, does modern evolution theory provide any difficulties for the view that there may be an actually transcendent God? Before we draw conclusions on this issue, we need to note that the problem of length of time was not the only difficulty with Darwin's idea of natural selection. The idea itself, even in our time, has remained the subject of intense discussion and debate.

Arguments in favour of Darwinian evolution theory refer to fossils in geological strata showing stages of development of many plants and animals. For example, the horse is traced from a four-toed, cat-sized creature. Thousands of studies of the structure, embryonic development, chemistry and geographic distribution of organisms are used to indicate the descent from common ancestors of widely differing species. Chemical and radioactive dating and other methods are used to show that life has been on earth for millions of years and the times at which various organisms evolved. The earliest fish has been dated back 500 million years, the earliest apes 25 million years ago, and modern humans some 50,000 years. In the 1890s, emphasis on Gregor Mendel's discoveries about the workings of genetics led to the neo-Darwinist or synthetic theory of evolution. This said that species evolve by means of natural selection. Yet they do so because of random mutations in the genetic make-up, not because of minor variations occurring between all the individual instances. Although some variations are destructive, others enable survival. So chance can be seen as acting with necessity in the production of plant and animal life. In 1986, Richard Dawkins published *The Blind Watchmaker*, in which he argues that evolution by natural selection as an unconscious random process is the only answer to why we exist. The only "watchmaker" in nature is "the blind forces of physics....Natural selection has...no purpose in mind." Dawkins thinks that if one does not opt for the "organic primeval soup" as the source of life on earth, there is also the theory of spontaneously arising self-replicating crystals. The enormous improbability of the original "start" he thinks could have come about as an event occurring only once in about a billion years, although he admits that we do not know how natural selection began on earth. The entire process of evolution comes about through cumulative selection in which the items in question are in a continuous process of selection over generations (Dawkins 1991, 5, 139-40, 143-46, 148, 150, 159, 162-65). Once the spontaneous start has occurred, mutation is the first stage in the evolution process, random in the sense of not pushing towards improvement. Natural selection is the second stage of the process, a non-random force, pushing towards improvement, but not with conscious purpose (Dawkins 1996, 76).

We can note here that the original Darwin notion of the struggle for survival has disappeared from neo-Darwinism. We are simply referred to features of the various plants and animals that do survive. We also need to be clear that there are many different views concerning natural selection, and the question has to be asked how far natural selection can provide a total explanation of evolution. For example, it may be only one element in the total explanation, and of course there are rival theories.—Gabriel Dover, professor of genetics at the University of Leicester, has pointed out that the majority of genetic and observable differences within and between species is non-Darwinian, because they have arisen either through accidents of drift, or as a consequence of several internal mechanisms of genetic turnover as embodied in the molecular drive theory of evolution (Dover 1993; see Milton 1992, ch. 17, esp. 191-94, 207-08).

Science writer Richard Milton is concerned at the way in which the neo-Darwinian theory of evolution is taught in schools as though it is concretely established fact rather than theory. Milton, in his book *The Facts of Life*, 1992, expresses his concern that Darwinists still cannot with certainty document the truth of the theory. Milton has problems with the age of the earth. Do we know that it is 4,600 million years old, and if it is, could this provide enough time for a Darwinian evolution? He also has difficulties with the time-scale and method of dating of the geological column and thinks that more attention needs to be paid to the role of natural catastrophe and the fact that radioactive dating methods are not as trustworthy as people think. The question of gaps in the fossil record also needs addressing adequately. On the question of spontaneous genetic mutation and natural selection, Milton points out that it is unclear why some characteristics should favour the survival of a particular animal such as the giraffe or cheetah. Milton is dubious about accounts of particular modern evolutionary changes, since e.g. in the case of the peppered moth in the Manchester area, there was a non-genetic solution to the survival of the dark species, namely, that birds spotted the lighter ones more easily and ate them. Milton raises the issue of problems of sterility and genetic homeostasis with respect to the limits of variation.[27] Finally, he is critical of Richard Dawkins. He thinks that time and distance cannot make something improbable probable, and that Dawkins tries to solve the problem of an impossible probability by putting together what Dawkins sees as a lot of less improbable tiny steps leading to the big improbability. This approach does not make a complex organ like the eye easier to come into being in Milton's view. While it is true that the minimum overall probability is a product of all the probabilities of the needed steps to the end, this does not lessen the improbability of each individual step when one takes into account the need for the correct sequence. One has to think about the probability of each step coming when it does (Milton 1992, 142-49). Note that Milton is not saying that the eye cannot possibly have evolved; he is simply saying that the improbability of the individual steps coming in the right order at the right time is as great as if one did a leap to the last step without the intermediate steps.

The above shows that the neo-Darwinistic theory of evolution by natural selection is by no means established fact, and that just because neo-Darwinism seems to some people to be the only possibility, this does not mean that one should not engage in in-depth investigation of the theory, such as that undertaken by Richard Milton. One should not close one's mind to the possibility of other options. Milton, whose arguments so far have received no serious scientific response, is not a closet creationist, his investigations resting entirely on his scientific research. Nor can we put all creationist arguments in one basket and reject every argument as naïve. Some are very weak, using a literalistic understanding of the Genesis creation narratives. Other arguments are strictly scientific and do not warrant a crass dismissal (Milton 1992, 13, 167; see Spong 1999, 35-38). As Milton points out, there are creationists today who view God as a creator God, but do not insist on a literal interpretation of the Genesis creation accounts. Scientific creationists, many of whom are Christians and scientists, interest

themselves not in the relation of neo-Darwinism to the Bible, but in
the extent to which scientific evidence casts doubt on the theory.

Does this mean then that evolution theory definitely does not rule
out the possibility of God's existence? Given our previous discussion,
the answer to this is fairly clear, namely that it does not. For the sake
of the argument, let us first assume that Richard Dawkins is absolutely
correct in all his neo-Darwinistic assumptions. Let us then note the
conclusion he draws from them. In *The Blind Watchmaker* (Dawkins
1991, 316-17) he rightly says that the creationist simply postulates
an intelligent and complex deity, and that one can just as well simply
postulate the existence of life as we know it. Dawkins is absolutely
correct to point to the problem of the metaphysical barrier, and that
an alternative philosophical option is that maybe all there is is the
universe. Yet Dawkins does not stop at an agnostic position. He seems
to assume that the physical universe is all we have and that there is
no divine power behind the universe. In other words, what is sauce
for the goose is sauce for the gander, since Dawkins, even though
he admits that one cannot disprove the existence of a divine power,
simply postulates that the physical universe is all that we have, with
the neo-Darwinistic theory of evolution and the feature of cumulative
natural selection as the only theory that in principle is able to explain
the existence of organized complexity. On the assumption, however,
that Richard Milton and others are correct in finding flaws with
neo-Darwinism, and especially noting Milton's criticism of Dawkins'
cumulative selection as a way of reducing the enormous statistical
improbability of the existence of life, Dawkins is left with a huge
improbability that is not removed by his version of neo-Darwinism.

The improbability problem that Dawkins faces is, of course, linked
to the fact of the fine-tuning needed in order for our universe to exist
with life in it. Paul Davies, as we have seen, considers the problem
of fine-tuning. He acknowledges the weakness of the Paley watch
argument. He also acknowledges that random mutations and natural
selection can be used as an alternative explanation. Yet he points to
the area where evolution theory cannot be used. For Darwin's theory
to work, there has to be a number of individual creatures in order that
selection can do its work. Davies argues that with the laws of physics
and the initial conditions at the start of the universe, we have only

what is unique to our universe. It makes no sense to speak in terms of laws of physics competing for survival (Davies 1992, 200-04, 213). Although on the multiverse theory (see endnote 7) one can speak of random occurrences of universes with different laws of physics, this is not the same, and it still, of course, does not provide an ultimate answer to the mystery of the existence of the universe.

A problem that also has to be faced is the advent of consciousness, self-consciousness, in the universe. Physicist James Jeans, who was also impressed by the fact that the universe seemed to show evidence of a designing or controlling power that had something in common with our own minds, thought the universe looked more like a great thought than anything mechanical. He suggested that the basis of the universe might be mind (Jeans 1930, 148-49). John Polkinghorne has pointed out that there is a puzzle needing solution about the relationship between consciousness and evolution. He does not see that evolution theory adequately answers the problem, and he thinks that those who emphasize the blindness of evolution are considering only the element of randomness, or what appears to be chance, at the expense of the element of natural law and what may be behind it. It is for this reason that he opts for dual-aspect monism as a means of including consciousness fully in the picture (Polkinghorne 1996a, 59, 64, 77). Paul Davies also considers the issue of the advent of consciousness. He thinks that if Darwinian evolution theory is accepted as a total explanation, then consciousness is a by-product of evolution's blind groping. If there is another explanation, then consciousness and intelligence could be seen as the natural product of "bio-friendly laws" (Davies & Adams 1998, 74-75). Some, such as Jacques Monod, see only free, blind, pure chance at the root of evolution (Monod 1972, 110). Yet with this we are back with the same problem that also dogged Alastair Hardy in his attempt to include mind in a Darwinian universe. The Darwinian model, taken on its own, without any presuppositions concerning ultimate origins of the universe, is a one-stuff model of the world. Hence it is difficult to include mind in it, except as a seeming by-product of the ongoing process. It is thus not surprising to find that religious scientists have attempted to apply the concept of evolution to include mind and religion. It is also interesting to note that Alfred Russel Wallace, fellow discoverer of the theory of evolution, became interested in the popular Spiritualism movement of the 1860s. He tried to work out a "scientific" explanation of how evolution worked through a mechanism involving a "superior being." Wallace thought that nature was guided and the process of evolution had a higher meaning, leading to an evolved form of life controlled by spirits from beyond our world. Darwin was dismayed at the development of Wallace's ideas, but it remains of interest that Wallace tried to account for the fact of parapsychological experience (White & Gribbin 1995, 233, 266; Clark 1984, 134-35).

(d) Concepts of Evolution

An early attempt to unite religion and evolution theory appears in the writings of Henry Drummond (1851-1897), who wrote *The Ascent of Man* in 1894. Drummond was a Free Church Minister and professor in natural science, an evolutionist, who declared that it was incorrect to speak of reconciling Christianity with evolution because the two were one. Drummond accepted the Darwinian idea of the struggle for life, but he also referred to a struggle for the life of others. The former struggle could be seen as essential to the evolutionary process because individuals had to compete for resources. But, Drummond argued, the struggle for the life of others was vital too. Once the human mind had evolved, self-sacrifice, co-operation, and maternal love would contribute to the survival of societies in which these virtues were encouraged.

Christianity and evolution were ultimately one, because both denoted a method of creation, both had the object of the making of more perfect beings. Altruistic love could be seen as essential to evolution and Christianity. Hence evolution could be seen as concerned with progress in both spirit and matter. In his book (Drummond 1896, vi-viii, 9, see esp. chs. I-IV, VI & X), Drummond explains that his aim is to trace the ascent of man, the individual, during the early stages of his evolution, up to his rise to family life. Drummond speaks of the evolution of evolution when spiritual laws evolve out of the natural laws. The natural evolutionary processes continue into the evolution of altruistic ethics, or ethical evolution. The struggle of the survival of the fittest becomes the struggle for others. Evolution is only the revelation of the infinite spirit, the eternal life returning to itself.

There seem to me to be some major difficulties with Drummond's view. The first is, it is unclear how he marries the traditional Christian universe with its notion of an actually transcendent God to Darwinistic evolution theory. Second, he seems to ascribe to natural evolution an inherent overall purpose, that of making more perfect beings. Yet such an assumption of purpose is a metaphysical one. The third problem is that evolution theory deals with what is apparently the state of affairs, how things are, and it is difficult to see how, in the course of evolution, altruism evolves from competition in nature, given that natural competition is self-oriented. To do this, one might have to posit that altruism is ultimately selfishness in disguise, or else, as T.H. Huxley did, see humans as operating from the sphere of culture and intellect and combating nature from an ethical perspective. Huxley, arguing that morality usually consists in doing precisely the opposite to that suggested by biology, said that "the ethical progress of Society depends, not on imitating the cosmic process...but in combating it" (Huxley T.S. & J.S. 1947, 82, 64). Drummond, however, was critical of Huxley on this issue, accusing him of turning his back on sub-human nature, whereas for Drummond a divine teleology was implicit in the entire evolutionary process (Drummond 1896, 26-32).

Richard Dawkins faces something of the same problem when he argues that living organisms exist for the benefit of DNA. For Dawkins, there is no implicit meaning to the universe and its events. All we have are genes propagating and managing to survive. Dawkins is famous for his book *The Selfish Gene*, in which the world of the selfish gene is one of savage competition that is selfish, even when it appears to be undertaking altruistic actions. Dawkins aims to show, therefore, that both individual selfishness and altruism can be explained by what he describes as the fundamental law of "gene selfishness." Genes are the chief policy makers because they dictate the way bodies and nervous systems are built, hence they indirectly exert control over behaviour, both selfish and altruistic. Dawkins sees brains taking over more and more control of actual decisions of policy, yet clearly, still in the service of survival. Despite this, Dawkins expresses the hope that perhaps the human race does have a capacity for genuine, disinterested, and hence true, altruism. He links this thought to his theory of "memes," ideological units that propagate in a competitive way in society and individual psyches (Dawkins 1991, 126; Dawkins 1989, 6, 60, 189-201 esp. 200, see 50, 59, 278-80). It is difficult to find this account of genes satisfactory. It is inherently reductive with respect to mind and culture, while at least some ideas are treated extremely reductively (see Polkinghorne 1996a, 111). Subjective purposive consciousness Dawkins views only as an object, as the culmination of the evolution of the capacity to simulate, even though he views why it happened as a mystery. The God meme, or God idea, is treated as a placebo used by humans in the light of the ills of the human race. Dawkins assumes that the idea of God is "copied" by successive generations of individual brains and has high survival value. He does not attempt to deal with the phenomenon of people's religious experiences, though on his view, one would surely have to regard them as some form of self-delusion or hallucination. Finally, such a position does not explain the view of someone like Søren Kierkegaard, who advocates celibacy as part of the extreme ideal of Christianity as renunciation of the world. For Kierkegaard, while marriage is permissible, it possesses an unavoidable self-orientation towards the family unit, hence, especially in a culture where marriage was regarded somewhat as a duty, he brushes aside the imagined complaints of people that if everyone renounced marriage the human race would become extinct (Kierkegaard 1967-78, III, L-R, entries 2621, 2623). It is hard to identify Kierkegaard's ideality as a competitive meme in any way contributing to the survival of the human race. Nor is Kierkegaard's thought about Christian ideality consoling. It is difficult to see how Dawkins could accommodate a Kierkegaard on his view, except on the theory that Kierkegaard was crazy or self-deluded in relation to a defective meme about a realm of actual divine transcendence.

A classic example of the attempt to unite the idea of evolution with religion, specifically Christianity, is to be found in the writings of pastor and scientist Pierre Teilhard de Chardin (1881-1955). Teilhard's view can be described as a religious Darwinism, since he starts from the materially evolved universe. His project as a scientist is to see and describe what he understands as a vast evolutionary process, in which simple entities build up into greater and greater complexities. The law of the process appears to be that with increasing complexity there is an increased movement towards life and consciousness. For Teilhard, there are critical moments in the process, when complexity arrives at the stage when some new condition comes about. Teilhard thinks that the idea of evolution, though observable only on our planet, can be applied to the universe as a whole. On earth, the great stages of change have been when life first appeared, then the advent of the self-conscious human race, something Teilhard calls "hominization." At this point, in addition to the physical features of earth, the advent of life initiates the "biosphere," and the arrival of self-consciousness initiates the "noosphere." Teilhard does not, however, stop here, since he posits the process converging on what he calls the "omega-point," a superpersonal unity of everything in God. On Teilhard's view, the deity is the end towards which all things are drawn to perfection in God. Jesus Christ is seen as the centre of the evolutionary process, an actualization of the final omega-point situation. Yet although Teilhard seems to indicate God is actually transcendent, he had difficulties in accommodating the notion of an actual divine transcendence to his view. In a letter to a friend, he wrote that he could not reconcile what he described as his pantheism with his faith as a Roman Catholic. In addition, whereas Teilhard succeeds in retaining the notion of evolutionary process, he can hardly be regarded as merely seeing and describing it. Clearly a lot of imaginative presuppositions of a metaphysical nature have smuggled themselves into his science, and we must note that the concept of process, in the idea of evolutionary process, seems, in his writings, to translate itself into the idea of progress (Teilhard de Chardin, 1965; Macquarrie 1971, 271-73; Molar 1967, 22-24; Huxley 1964, 206-21; see Tipler 1994, 110-16).

This notion of process as progress appears in the work of Frank J. Tipler, who, reusing Teilhard de Chardin's concept of an "omega point," attempts a scientific prognostication of the end of things. On his view, humans consciously intervene in the Darwinian process, and the essence of life (information) is ultimately saved by artificial intelligence, which would become the advanced minds able to cope with the ultimate death of the physical universe. Teilhard de Chardin's "omega point" would thus be achieved, but in a form unthought of by Teilhard. In Tipler's ultimate universe, all life and all humans are resurrected in a computer universe (since the essence of humans in Tipler's view is also information) and have a kind of physicalist eternal life (Tipler 1994, 218; see Polkinghorne 1996a, 97-99). Tipler's scenario presents us with a physicalist version of divine design and a somewhat materialistic "life after death" scenario for humans. In a sense he remains within a one-stuff Darwinian universe and hence has no problems concerning transcendent divinities, but he, too, seems to let his imagination run away with his science. Apart from any other considerations (such as the quality of the scientific explanation of his theory), he presupposes that evolution entails positive progress towards an excellent end.

The above may serve as a warning, when studying the theory of evolution, not to import presuppositions, especially metaphysical ones, into Darwinism or to fasten on to a feature of the theory and use it to explain some or all aspects of human existence. A prime example of the latter is that of Ernst Haeckel in Germany, who, in mixing Darwinism with his own ideas, inadvertently helped to influence the ideology of fascism through his confused fusion of sociology and his misunderstanding of Darwin's theory. Haeckel's thinking helped bring about the rise of Social Darwinism as a pseudo-science, Social Darwinism applying the notion of the struggle for existence to society seen as being in a state of egoistic struggle for existence. The fittest, the strongest, were viewed as surviving, with "might making right." Social selection was thus considered to operate in society just as natural selection operated in nature.[28]

A factor of interest with reference to attempts to develop Darwinian evolution theory is thus that the notion of process very easily seems to slip into the idea of progress, such that everything is seen as developing into something better than the previous version. Either the betterment is seen in terms of survival value, or it is seen as some kind of inherent betterment going on in the system until self-consciousness and culture are reached. It is not clear, however, that survival value is necessarily beneficial for other creatures who may get wiped out by the stronger creatures. That the extinction of dinosaurs is said to have enabled mammals to flourish is not an argument that it was "better" for mammals to survive and not dinosaurs, since one could mount an argument that the human race as one of the end-products poses a threat to life on the planet and thus also to itself. Nor, from the standpoint of evolution theory, can one see that the advent of self-consciousness is "better" than plant life or instinctive consciousness, especially when it has enabled humans to make destructive things like atom bombs. Hence evolution theory in any form cannot be made to do too much. Where Darwinian evolution theory is concerned, it most certainly cannot support ideas of development as progress in the sense of betterment. All it can do is to be a theory that people can test against observations of the biological situation of the world.

(e) An Unintended Red Herring

Historian, philosopher, and Darwinist Michael Ruse, in his book *The Darwinian Paradigm* (Ruse 1993, 146-54), raises the issue of teleology—"end-directed thinking and language" about biological life. He points out that "function" and "purpose" language where plants and organisms are concerned are used with reference to survival and reproduction, but that the question still needs to be asked how appropriate teleological language is in the field of biology. In the period immediately prior to Darwin, teleology in biology was evidence of the divine creator. After Darwin, teleological language was with reference to the struggle for existence, and to successful survival characteristics carried on to the next generation. Any presupposed divine creativity therefore had to be presupposed as occurring a step back, the creator using the processes of natural selection. Yet with reference to consciousness, a goal-directed teleology can be seen as appearing, for example, in the intentional behaviour of chimpanzees. Ruse also points to non-conscious examples of goal-directed behaviour such as mechanisms for keeping bird-clutch sizes at an optimum number. The mechanisms are teleological in the local sense of natural selection, although some ornithologists may treat them additionally in terms of goal-directed teleology.

As Ruse also points out, the line between organic and inorganic matter can no longer be sharply drawn, since molecules and atoms are at the basis of both, and there is now a science of molecular genetics. He asks whether such developments in biology will mean the end of the application of teleological thinking to biology. Ruse, however, agreeing that there can be non-teleological explanations of goal-directedness with respect to organic phenomena, sees a place also for teleological analysis. For Ruse, whatever the factual case may be, organisms seem as if they were designed. To drop a teleological approach would be to ignore the design-like feature of living matter, a view Ruse sees as reinforced by molecular genetics with its emphasis on the end-fixated nature of organic life. Finally, Ruse considers the extent of the apparent design in the natural world. He argues that although not every aspect of an organism can be seen as functioning towards the overall benefit of an organism, this does not mean it does not have a function or that an end-directed understanding can be eliminated. Indeed, in research, biologists use teleological models to show how organisms might best be expected to use their resources, and then check their models against nature with very successful results.

When we reach the sphere of teleology with respect to human consciousness and morals, and consideration of morality in terms of evolution, Ruse considers the two levels of the command to love in the New Testament, finding that Darwinian evolution theory can accommodate the ordinary level of neighbour love, since it can be argued that people are better off in survival terms if they cooperate. With the stronger command concerning love, however, such as loving one's enemies, and loving everyone without apparently making distinctions between family, friends, and enemies, Ruse sees that there is a problem for the Darwinist, in that loving everyone in this manner does not accord with the mechanisms of kin selection and with community-building reciprocal altruism. Secondly, with the notion of unlimitedly being willing to endure an affront when wronged by someone, the biological need for reciprocation must rule out the unlimited scope of such a demand. Ruse points out that moral sense produced by evolution could not require such behaviour, since natural selection could not find much use for such a principle. So for Ruse, the stronger version of Christian ethics conflicts with the implications of modern evolutionary thought. For the Darwinian evolutionist, morality is merely an aid to survival and reproduction and nothing more. Ruse concludes that if we follow through the implications of modern Darwinian evolution theory, the evolutionist and the Christian part company. For the Darwinian evolutionist, the Christian has a biological illusion of objectivity, whereas the Christian sees morality as resting on ultimate and non-Darwinian foundations.[29] Christianity (and any religion with a similar strict love ethic) calls for humans to rise above natural self-orientation and the desire for the survival of anything we include in the sphere of the self (Ruse 1993, 250-72).

It should be noted that Ruse is not arguing that Darwinism proves God does not exist. All he is claiming is that in his view, neo-Darwinism is "good tough science" (Ruse 1987, xiii, 207-72; Ruse 1993, 266), and he is showing that Darwinism cannot accommodate Christian ethics taken at their highest level of ideality. Similarly, with his discussion of apparent design and teleology in the natural world, he is considering design in what one might call local this-worldly manifestations. He is not using it to presuppose, like Paul Davies for instance, that a divine intelligence is steering things. Darwinism cannot be used to prove or disprove the existence of a divine power behind things, since it is concerned with biological life in the world and not with metaphysical issues. On the Darwinian view, the weaker version of Christian and similar morality comes about in societies as part of the survival process. Extreme world-denying moralities, since they cannot be proved by science to have an other-worldly foundation of any kind, simply cannot come into the evolutionary picture.

I have not been able to consider alternative versions and modifications of Darwinism in this book, first, because it would take a book in itself, second, because I am not qualified, and such discussion is best left to qualified scientists. Third, in the light of the concept of the theme of this book, it is not necessary, since those using Darwinism in any way on the religious front, or against the religious front, seem to think only in terms of neo-Darwinism, so I would like to conclude here by suggesting, in the light of the above, that the Darwinian theory of evolution has become an unintended red herring in discussion about God's existence. It seems to me that the entire issue of Darwinism is tremendously complex, and that one cannot rule out that it might suffer the same kind of revolution as happened with Newtonian physics in relation to the advent of relativity theory. Indeed, we already have the neo-Darwinian revision of Darwin's original theory. Just as literalist creationists ought not to be afraid of looking at the Genesis narratives with a more open understanding of truth, so, too, should Darwinists always maintain an open view in relation to the theory and be ready to provide serious answers to scientific objections to the theory. The temptation to use Darwinism either as some kind of proof or disproof of the existence of a divine power should definitely be resisted, since this is simply not science. Whether or not one believes in a divine power, one should not go along with the urge to use Darwinism in some way to reinforce what one sees as the rightness of what is one's metaphysical belief. Despite a plenitude of serious writers on the subject, there are still too many ready with a triumphal dismissal of opposing views. For some, the desire to dismiss the idea of God's existence, or to assert the existence of a particular God concept, is such that the tone of the language used tends to become non-scholarly and derisive of other opinions, and when and where this occurs it is to be regretted.

In his book, *A Rumour of Angels* (Berger 1971, 42, 52, 62-63, 70-96, 104), sociologist Peter Berger argues that people need to liberate themselves from the assumptions of their time. He sees that each conception of the world, irrespective of its objective truth, will be plausible to the individual in relation to the strength of the supporting structure. He thinks the situation of religious pluralism in our world forces the individual to choose, and it makes religious certainty hard to come by. This is particularly the case in our time when there is no dearth of voices claiming that their particular vision of the divine or of the universe is the only correct and complete one. Berger quotes the German historian Leopold von Ranke's saying that "each age is immediate to God." With this, Ranke aims to reject the notion of progress that treats the current present moment as the pinnacle of history. Berger sees sociology as helping us to liberate ourselves from the apparent certitudes of our time. He also thinks the idea that religion is a human product or projection can be stood on its head.[30] Giving some examples, Berger thinks that those writing about theological issues should seek "signals of transcendence" (from all traditions), phenomena from our human situation that point beyond it. He also calls for revival of the spirit of patient induction, together with an attitude of openness to all human experience, both present and historical.

Conclusion

I return to the cathedral square in the city of Copenhagen. I deliberately did not set out to argue that there was a supernature and an actual divine transcendence, because this, as I have tried to show, is an impossible task. I hope, however, I may have achieved my more modest goal of making clear that those who believe there is a supernature and an actual divine transcendence have no reason to cast aside their view just because there are theologians and scientists wishing to dismiss such an idea as "not modern." We may know a lot in our century, but there is still very much we do not know, and we need always to bear in mind that there is a metaphysical barrier. We must be careful to do our best to make a distinction between ideas and views we hold on the basis of belief and religious faith, and those that are genuinely so solidly grounded in science that they are indisputable. In many ways this book cannot avoid being superficial, a caricature of what could be said on the subject, but I hope the few thoughts that I present may work in the same way as a caricature, namely, by making the essential features stand out. I would be very happy if my thoughts in any way relieved someone from being imprisoned in restrictive concepts of any kind that may work against the life of that person viewed, if I may use such an "old-fashioned" term, as a spiritual being.

Acknowledging the fact of human conflicts with respect to forms of religiosity, I personally presuppose an actually transcendent divine power capable of communicating with the individual in many ways. As I have tried to indicate, the idea of such a transcendent power does not mean that individual conceptions of the divine are purely subjective, especially when the form of the divine power is manifested in a historical figure as opposed to a metaphysical one. (Hence on the view that allows for an actual transcendence, the historical Jesus continues to live in the eternal realm and prayer can be addressed to him). What it means is that the divine manifests itself to the individual in a mode understandable to that individual. I also think there need be no conflict between the notion of God as personal or as totally impersonal. People do experience God as personal, though it is unfortunate that in some religious traditions a masculine label has been so heavily attached to the concept of God, a situation not remedied by trying to get people to accept a feminine notion of the divine personality as a replacement image. It might be helpful if we could try to think of "personal" here more in terms of conscious divine response than in terms of human sexuality, bearing in mind that there is a sense in which the divine power is above notions of personality (as is expressed

in religious traditions without the concept of God). As Huston Smith
has pointed out (Smith 1992, 52-53, 86-87, 90-91), there is a sense in
which God as "Godhead" transcends all descriptions in what he calls
a "transpersonal mode," a happier phrase than the word "impersonal"
with its connotations of indifference.[31]

From all this it is clear that there is nothing wrong in recognizing and
accepting what speaks to you, concerning the divine power, bearing
in mind the duty to be critical and not accept destructive or nonsen-
sical pseudo-religions, negative cults and ideologies, such as Hitler's
encouragement of a Wagnerian inspired pseudo-religion to buttress
Nazism (with himself as messianic redeemer), or Jim Jones' religious
colony in Guyana (SBS Australia 1996; Time 1978, 6-14). Søren Kierkegaard acknowledged by faith a transcendent God, incarnated in
Jesus, an eternal power that also omnipresently pervaded all existence;
a heavenly realm of God and life after death (see Watkin 1997). For
Matthew Arnold, God was the "Eternal not ourselves that makes for
righteousness" (Arnold 1970, 157). Paul Tillich wanted to transcend
the theistic idea of God, equating God with Being itself, using terms
such as "ground" and "power" of being (Tillich 1962, 174-76). Yet,
as I have attempted to point out in these pages, we are not justified
in using our understandings of the divine power to assert as certainty
the rightness of a particular metaphysical position, a particular picture
of God, especially where this concerns the actual state of affairs in the
universe. If one thinks, despite all the evidence, that God created the
world in six days and this is important to one's belief structure, that
is one thing; it is another when one wants everyone else to opt for a
literal understanding of the Genesis creation narratives. If one thinks
this world and this life is all there is and chooses to live by such an
assumption, that is one thing; it is quite another when there is an
attempt to force this assumption on others, or to declare belief in an
actually transcendent divine power to be old-fashioned nonsense.

Walking in the cathedral square of Copenhagen, I pass the bust of
Niels Bohr, pausing a respectful moment to acknowledge his enormous
contribution to our understanding of the universe. I come to the
doorway of the bishop's palace: "Thi vort Borgerskab er i himlene"—
"We...are citizens of heaven." I am happy to acknowledge this as my
fundamental citizenship. By faith it has always been my citizenship,

because it corresponds to my life's experience and understanding of the way things are. I do not want to inflict my standpoint on pastor Grosbøll, or on any who think differently, but to my last breath I will reject pseudo modern (and "postmodern") metaphysical assumptions and assertions put forward as the definitive truth to which I am supposed (in both senses of the word) to subscribe.

Notes

[1] Grosbøll rejects the worldview of a distant time, and wishes to separate God as interpretation from God as explanation. He states that: "the God of...transcendence is dead," "to love God is to love God in one's neighbour...only in him do we recognize God," "God is dead, and that is good." "God is indeed dead, but his grave is here." "The words of the creed represent precisely all that we can't bring ourselves to say. Pure abracadabra." "We don't believe in God and not at all as the creator of heaven and earth or as almighty...." (Grosbøll 2003b, 10, 42-43, 54, 71, 90, 113, 147-48). I omit his rejection of most of the credal statements about Jesus because I am here concerned only with Grosbøll's view of God. (Please note that all secular Danish translations in this book are my own).

[2] On May 16, 2004, Grosbøll preached a sermon in which he repeated the same kind of statements for which he had previously (3.6.03) been suspended and then allowed to return to his parish (23.7.03) under close scrutiny. He was again suspended (3.6.04) and given the choice (9.6.04) of resigning his pastorate or being taken to court for civil and doctrinal dereliction of duty, since a pastor in the national (Danish Lutheran) church is also a civil servant.

[3] Matthew Arnold's 1867 poem "Dover Beach," speaks of the decline of "the sea of faith" (Arnold 1922, 401-02).

[4] In traditional Christian theology, God is viewed as immanent, in that the divine energy is seen as flowing into all the operations of living creatures, and God indwells in the souls of the just. God is also viewed as transcendent, meaning superior to, and independent of, the world, the divine creator (see Aquinas 1963, Prima Pars, 1 a. Vol 2: The Existence and Nature of God, Question 8 Articles 1-4: God's Existence in things. Also Thomas Gilby in appendix 14: Transcendence 1 a 7 and Immanence 1 a 8. See also Scruton 1994, 121; Spong 1999, 130).

[5] For a good diagram showing an early conception of the universe, see Bible 1954, 162.

⁶ It should be noted, however, that Hawking, whose later view of the universe as self-contained seems to have no place for a God, finds it hard to let go of the God word, at least as the answer in physics to why the universe bothers to exist (Hawking 1993a, 172-73). See also Colin Goodwin (Goodwin 1996) for a clear exposition of Hawking's earlier and later view of the universe. Peter Atkins also opts for a theory of everything, but he stresses chance as the originator of things (Atkins 1994, 107, 133), whereas, with Hawking's self-originating universe via quantum fluctuation, the theory of everything seems to be the prime feature of things.

⁷ See also Davies 1992, chs. 7-9 for Davies' detailed discussion, also Davies & Adams 1996, 138-51. John Leslie concludes that either God is real and/or there exist an enormous number of varied universes (Leslie 1996, 204). In a number of TV programmes (ABC Australia 2000, BBC Two 2002, ABC Australia 2002, ABC Australia 2004) scientists claim that an updated theory of parallel universes in a multi-universe or "multiverse" solves all problems about the origin of the universe. They argue that there could be an infinite number of parallel universes each with a different law of physics. Matter is seen to be made up of strings attached to a membrane; there are 11 dimensions. Big bangs that start universes are caused by the collision of parallel universes in the sea of membrane universes. Time can now be traced back to before the big bang, and there is no longer a singularity problem at the beginning of our universe where the laws of physics cannot be applied. So the grand unified theory or theory of everything, uniting the four forces of existence (weak and strong nuclear forces, electromagnetism and gravity) has been achieved. The TV programmes want to suggest that our universe is nothing more than one of an infinite number of membranes, one of the many universes in the multiverse. Assuming this theory is correct, the metaphysical barrier is, however, still there. No one can explain why there should be a super universe or anything. It can be noted that an Australian-led research team in January 2004 discovered a string of galaxies that, it is said, call for a reexamination of theories about how the universe was formed (Examiner 2004). We simply do not know everything. "Everything," taken literally, moves one into

metaphysics, while there are still a mass of unanswered questions concerning many finite things.

[8] Bishop and philosopher George Berkeley (1685-1753) is, of course, famous for his presentation of idealism, rejecting a material universe (Berkeley 1992).

[9] According to one's perception of the universe, one may, of course, be a panentheist, viewing the universe as part, but not all, of God, or one may see God as the soul of the universe in the view known as panexperientialism.

[10] John Hick also makes this point (Goulder & Hick 1983, 32). For those wishing to explore this topic further, two very helpful works are Barbour 1966 and Barbour 1990.

[11] Crain thinks Peacocke's model does not seem to exclude the possibility of divine intervention interfering with natural laws (See Peacocke 1993, 135-83). Peacocke (182-83) is cautious about miracles. Like Reginald Fuller (see my chapter 3 (d)), Peacocke thinks we need to assess historical evidence. He also thinks one's assessment is going to be influenced by one's view of the universe and of the possibility of miracles.

[12] We should perhaps remind ourselves here that one needs to be very careful before applying ideas of God to forms of Buddhism, though Huston Smith argues that the concept of Nirvana can be regarded as the concept of God as Godhead. Smith also makes an interesting link between the Buddhist idea and Paul Tillich's notion of the "God above God" (Smith 1991, 114-15, 151 n. 34; Tillich 1962, 180-83).

[13] On the topic of religious experience, pioneers before Hardy are, of course, Edwin Starbuck and William James (Starbuck 1899; James 1977). In the field of parapsychology Rosalind Heywood also has done pioneering work (Heywood 1971; Heywood 1966).

[14] In this context, C. Stephen Evans provides an excellent discussion of religious experience (Evans 1985, ch. 4).

[15] On the debate concerning the nature of mind/consciousness see e.g. Dennett 1991; Churchland 1988; Chalmers 1996; Polkinghorne 1996a, ch. 5, esp. 61. Polkinghorne thinks that we need to refine talk of the soul so that it accords with the nature of reality; the soul is to be seen as one's real self, actuating the body.

[16] For a detailed discussion of the development of ideas of resurrection in Judaism and Christianity, see Coward 1997, chs. 1 & 2. We can also note the traditional Roman Catholic doctrine of purgatory, which says that it is "the place and state in which souls suffer for a while and are purged after death, before they go to Heaven, on account of their sins." (Attwater 1949, 413).

[17] On some of the major religions, see Armstrong 1993.

[18] Where humans are concerned, there is of course a risk that one can be so indirect with such a tactic that (especially when one is discussing a broad area, and with the passage of time) people fail to see what one is driving at. Hence Kierkegaard left, along with his huge and complex authorship, a report of his teaching method and his reasons for using it (Kierkegaard 1998b, Part Two, Ch. One).

[19] There may possibly be a similar puzzle concerning Spong on life after death. He lets us understand he believes in life after death, yet tells us that the human race is not eternal (Spong 1999, 228, 201, 210, 97).

[20] In the first edition of *Miracles* 1947, ch. 3, "The Self-Contradiction of the Naturalist," Lewis attempted to prove that human reason is independent of the natural world, only to have his arguments successfully savaged by Catholic philosopher Elizabeth Anscombe. Lewis revised this chapter as "The Cardinal Difficulty of Naturalism" in the 1960 edition of his book (Lewis 1974, 103-04; Carter 1981, 216-17; Anscombe 1948, 7-15).

[21] There is, not surprisingly, a vast literature on Hume and on the topic of miracles generally. See, for example, Williams 1990; Smart 1964, 25-49; Houston 1994; Grey 1993, 100-05; Swinburne 1970; Swinburne 1989, 446-53; Swinburne 1996, 114-39; Fogelin 2003.

[22] There is a slightly comic element to this story, in that I remember clearly that the member of staff for applications had on his desk a sign that said: "The impossible we do at once. Miracles take a little longer."

[23] Chapter One v. 1 to chapter Two v. 4 a: written by P, the Priestly writer [Jewish priestly circles in Exile, ca. 550 B.C.]. Chapter Two v. 4b to end of chapter 4: written by J, the Jahwist or Yahwist writer ["Yahwist" because the author used "Yahweh" to refer to God—ca. 950 B.C.]. In the 5th or 6th century B.C., there was a fusion of

J [by then already fused with material written by E, the Elohist, a writer who used "Elohim" to refer to God]. What has been known as JEDP was the final result, an interwoven narrative of all these sources. It should be noted that the Bible contains different types of material, thus it is important not to put the material under any one generalizing label.—I provide the summaries of the two creation accounts, because in my teaching experience I have found that one cannot be sure these days that everyone knows the stories.

24 The habit of using the diversity of Bible texts in a literal manner to "prove" various theological and other assumptions can here be questioned, but it also needs to be asked whether a divine inspiration mediated through Bible texts is something that can be mediated to the individual when the text is used as a conceptual tool rather than allowed to speak to the individual.

25 Darwinist biologist and philosopher Thomas Henry Huxley (1825-1895) was an agnostic who tended in the direction of atheism in that he saw the contents of the universe in terms of material forces and thought science was not yet able to decide the question of God's existence. For Huxley, states of consciousness, including volitions, were merely by-products of the workings of the brain.

26 Darwin's grandfather Erasmus Darwin (1731-1802) had, however, published his *Zoonomia; or the Laws of Organic Life* 1794-96, a forerunner of evolution theory, and Robert Chambers (1802-71) caused a stir in 1844 with his anonymously published, and scientifically imprecise, *Vestiges of the Natural History of Creation*. Chambers argued that humans and the human mind, together with all life, must be included within the workings of the laws of nature.

27 Milton 1992. The entire book needs careful consideration, but I emphasize here chs. 2-14, and see 4, 12-13, 16, 27, 49, 74, 124-29, 133-34, 139-46, 162-63, 171, 181, 191, 201, 216-17, 220-28, in relation to these points.

28 Michael Ruse (Ruse 1987, 78-93) provides an excellent analysis and critique of Social Darwinism.

29 Kierkegaard is able to accommodate altruism on his view since he has a dualistic perspective on the universe. The divine realm and the human realm are separate spheres. The human realm in its ordinary workings is naturally self-centred, and only the Christian

authentically imitating Christ is capable of genuine world-renouncing altruism (Kierkegaard 1967-78, IV, S-Z, entries 4238, 4501).

30 Ludwig Feuerbach, in his famous 1841 work *Das Wesen des Christentums* [The Essence of Christianity] (Feuerbach 1957), had claimed that religion was a giant human projection. He thus inverted Hegel's view of humans in conversation with God, so that what Hegel had seen as dialogue became, in Feuerbach's view, a human monologue.

31 See Bede Griffiths (Griffiths 1992, 69-71) for both an ultimate ground or reality of the universe and the concept of a personal God in Hinduism.

Bibliography

Books:

Altizer, Thomas J.J. & William Hamilton: *Radical Theology and the Death of God*, Harmondsworth: Penguin Books, 1968.

Anonymous: *The Cloud of Unknowing and other works*, translated into modern English by Clifton Wolters, Harmondsworth: Penguin Classics, Penguin Books, 1961, 1978.

Appleyard, Bryan: *Understanding the Present*, London: Picador/Pan Books, 1992.

Aquinas Thomas: *Summa Theologica*, Cambridge: Blackfriars, with London & New York: Eyre and Spottiswood and the McGraw-Hill Book Co., 1963.

Armstrong, Karen: *A History of God*, London: Heinemann, 1993.

Arnold, Matthew: Matthew Arnold, *God and the Bible*, vol. 7 in *The Complete Prose Works of Matthew Arnold*, ed. R.H. Super, Ann Arbor: University of Michigan Press, 1970.

————: *The Poems of Matthew Arnold 1840-1867*, London:Humphrey Milford, Oxford University Press, 1922.

Atkins, Peter: *Creation Revisited*, Harmondsworth: Penguin Books, 1994.

Attwater, Donald, ed.: *The Catholic Encyclopædic Dictionary*, London: Cassell and Co. 1949.

Balle, Nikolai Edinger: *Lærebog i den Evangelisk-christelige Religion indrettet til Brug i de danske Skoler* [Catechism in the Evangelical-Christian Religion for use in Danish Schools]. Copenhagen: 1791. (Available in Danish and English on the internet).

Ballou, Robert O.: *The Pocket World Bible*, London: Routledge & Kegan Paul, 1948.

Barbour, Ian: *Issues in Religion and Science*, London: SCM Press, 1966.

————: *Religion and Science*, San Francisco: HarperSanFrancisco, 1997.

————: *Religion in an Age of Science*, London: SCM Press, 1990.

Barrow, John D.: *Pi in the Sky*, Oxford: Clarendon Press, 1992.

———— & Frank J. Tipler: *The Anthropic Cosmological Principle*, Oxford: Oxford University Press, 1986.

Berger, Peter: *A Rumour of Angels. Modern Society and the Rediscovery of the Supernatural*, Harmondsworth: Penguin Books, 1971.

Berkeley, George: *A Treatise concerning the Principles of Human Knowledge*, in M.R. Ayers: George Berkeley: *Philosophical Works*, London & Rutland, Vermont: J.M. Dent & sons & Charles E. Tuttle: Everyman's Library, 1975, 1992.

The Bible, London: British & Foreign Bible Society, 1954, 1966.

Revised English Bible with the Apocrypha. Oxford: Oxford University Press, 1989.

Bjerg, Svend & Palle Steffensen: *Nedlæg folkekirken* [*Close the National Church*], Copenhagen: Høst & Søn, 2003.

Boslough, John: *Stephen Hawking's Universe*, London: Fontana/Collins, 1989.

Brooke, John Hedley: *Science and Religion, Some Historical Perspectives*, Cambridge: Cambridge University Press, 1991.

Capra, Fritjof: *The Tao of Physics*, London: Flamingo, Fontana Paperbacks, 1983.

Carter, Humphrey: *The Inklings*, London: Unwin Paperbacks, 1981.

Chalmers, David J. : *The Conscious Mind*, Oxford University Press, 1996.

Charlesworth, Max: *Religious Inventions: Four Essays*, Cambridge & New York: Cambridge University Press, 1997.

Churchland, Paul M.: *Matter and Consciousness*, Cambridge, MA: MIT Press, 1988.

Clark, Ronald W.: *The Survival of Charles Darwin*, London: Weidenfeld and Nicolson, 1984.

Coward, Harold, ed.: *Life after Death in World Religions*, Maryknoll, NY: Orbis Books, Faith Meets Faith Series, 1997.

Cupitt, Don: *The World to Come*, London: SCM Press, 1982.

Daniken, Erich von: *Chariots of the Gods,* London: Souvenir Press, 1969.

Darwin, Charles: *The Origin of Species* (first edition), Ware, Hertfordshire: Wordsworth Editions Limited, 1998.

————: *The Origin of Species* (2nd edition) in *The Origin of Species and The Descent of Man,* New York: The Modern Library, Random House, year of publication not given.

Davies, Paul: *God and the New Physics,* Harmondsworth: Penguin Books, 1984.

————: *The Mind of God,* London: Simon & Schuster, 1992.

———— with Phillip Adams: *The Big Questions,* Harmondsworth: Penguin Books, 1996.

———— with Phillip Adams: *More Big Questions,* Sydney: ABC Books, 1988.

Dawkins, Richard: *Climbing Mount Improbable,* London: Viking, Penguin Books, 1996.

————: *The Blind Watchmaker,* Harmondsworth: Penguin Books, 1991.

————: *The Selfish Gene,* Oxford: Oxford University Press, 1989.

Dawson, Christopher: *Progress and Religion An Historical Enquiry,* London: Sheed & Ward, 1945.

Dennett, Daniel: *Consciousness Explained,* Boston: Little, Brown, 1991.

Denton, Michael: *Evolution: A Theory in Crisis,* Bethesda, MD: Adler & Adler, 1985.

Descartes, René: *Meditations on First Philosophy,* in John Cottingham and others: *Descartes Selected Philosophical Writings,* Cambridge: Cambridge University Press, 1988.

Desmond, Adrian and James Moore: *Darwin. The Life of a Tormented Evolutionist,* New York: W.W. Norton, 1991.

Drummond, Henry: *The Ascent of Man,* London: Hodder and Stoughton, 1896.

Evans, C. Stephen: *Philosophy of Religion, Thinking about Faith,* Downers Grove, IL: InterVarsity Press, 1985.

Feuerbach, Ludwig: *The Essence of Christianity,* tr. George Eliot, New York: Harper & Row, Torchbook edition, 1957.

Fogelin, Robert J.: *A Defense of Hume on Miracles*, Princeton: Princeton University Press, 2003.

Fuller, Reginald H.: *Interpreting the Miracles*, London: SCM Press, 1963.

Gandhi, Mahatma: *All Men are Brothers*, New York: Columbia University Press, 1958.

Ghéon, Henri: *The Secret of the Curé D'Ars*, London: Sheed & Ward, 1946.

Gish, Duane: *Evolution – The Fossils Say No!* San Diego: Creation-Life Publishers, 1978.

Gosse, Edmund: *Father and Son*, Harmondsworth: Penguin Books, Penguin Classics 1986.

Gosse, Philip: *Omphalos*. 1857.

Goulder, Michael & John Hick: *Why Believe in God?* London: SCM Press, 1983.

Grosbøll, Thorkild: *En sten i skoen* [*A Stone in One's Shoe*], Copenhagen: Forlaget Anis, 2003.

Haeckel, Ernst: *The Riddle of the Universe* 1900. Translated by Joseph McCabe in Great Minds Series, Tucson, AZ: Galen Press, reprint, 1992.

Hardy, Alister: *The Divine Flame. An Essay Towards a Natural History of Religion*, London & Glasgow: Collins, 1966.

————: *The Spiritual Nature of Man*, Oxford: Clarendon Press, 1979. Mowbray/Cassell, 1990.

Hawking, Stephen: *A Brief History of Time*, New York: Bantam Press, 1988.

————: *Black Holes and Baby Universes*, New York: Bantam Press, 1993.

Hay, David: *Exploring Inner Space. Is God still Possible in the Twentieth Century?* London: Mowbray, revised ed. 1987.

————: *Religious Experience Today. Studying the Facts*, London: Mowbray/Cassell, 1990.

Heywood, Rosalind: *The Infinite Hive* (1964), London: Pan Books, 1966.

————: *The Sixth Sense* (1959), London: Pan Books, 1971.

Hick, John: John Hick: *Death and Eternal Life*, London: Collins, 1976.

————:*Evil and the God of Love*, London: Collins Fontana Library, 1968.

————: *Philosophy of Religion*, Englewood Cliffs, NJ: Prentice Hall, 4th ed. 1990.

Houston, J.: *Reported Miracles*, Cambridge: Cambridge University Press, 1994.

Huxley, Aldous: *The Devils of Loudon*, New York: Carroll and Graf Publishers, 1986.

Huxley, T.H. and J.S.: *Evolution and Ethics*, London: Pilot Press, 1947.

James, William: *The Varieties of Religious Experience, a study in Human Nature*, Gifford Lectures 1901-02. London: Collins Fount Paperbacks, 1977.

Jeans, James: *The Mysterious Universe*, Cambridge: Cambridge University Press, 1930.

Kee, Alister: *The Way of Transcendence. Christian Faith without Belief in God.* Harmondsworth: Penguin Books, 1971.

Keightley, Alan: *Wittgenstein, Grammar and God*, London: Epworth Press, 1976.

Kent, John H.S.: *The End of the Line? The Development of Christian Theology in the Last Two Centuries*, Minneapolis: Fortress Press edition, 1982.

————: *The Unacceptable Face. The Modern Church in the Eyes of the Historian,* London: SCM Press, 1987.

Kierkegaard, Søren: *The Book on Adler*, ed. & tr. Howard and Edna Hong, Princeton: Princeton University Press, 1998.

————: *Concluding Unscientific Postscript*, (1846), 1-2, ed. & tr. Howard & Edna Hong, Princeton: Princeton University Press, 1992.

————: *Fear and Trembling*, in *Fear and Trembling* [and] *Repetition*, ed. & tr. Howard and Edna Hong, Princeton: Princeton University Press, 1983.

————: *The Point of View*, ed. & tr. Howard and Edna Hong, Princeton: Princeton University Press, 1998.

————: *The Sickness unto Death*, ed. & tr. Howard & Edna Hong, Princeton: Princeton University Press, 1980.

————: *Upbuilding Discourses in Various Spirits*, ed. & tr. Howard & Edna Hong, Princeton: Princeton University Press, 1993.

————: *Works of Love*, ed. & tr. Howard & Edna Hong, Princeton: Princeton University Press, 1995.

————: *Søren Kierkegaard's Journals and Papers*, 7 vols. ed. & tr. Howard & Edna Hong, Bloomington and London: Indiana University Press, 1967-1978.

Kuhn, Thomas: *The Structure of Scientific Revolutions*, Chicago: University of Chicago Press, 1996.

Laurentin, René: *Bernadette of Lourdes*, London: Darton, Longman & Todd, 1979.

Leslie, John: *Universes*, London: Routledge, 1996.

Lewis, C.S.: *The Abolition of Man*, London: Collins Fount Paperbacks, 1978.

————: *The Last Battle*, Harmondsworth: Puffin Books and Bodley Head, 1964.

————: *Miracles*, London: Geoffrey Bles, 1947.

————: *Miracles*, (revised edition), London: Collins Fount Paperbacks, 1974.

————: *Surprised by Joy*, London: Collins Fount Paperbacks, 1977.

————: *Timeless at Heart*, London: Collins Fount Paperbacks, 1987.

Macquarrie, John: *Twentieth Century Religious Thought*, London: SCM Press, 1971.

Milton, Richard: *The Facts of Life, Shattering the Myth of Darwinism*. London: Fourth Estate, 1992.

Mivart, St. George Jackson: *On the Genesis of Species*. London & New York, 1871.

Molyneux, Georgina: *The Curé D'Ars: A Memoir of Jean-Baptiste-Marie Vianney*, London: Richard Bentley, 1869.

Monod, Jacques: *Chance and Necessity: An Essay on the Natural Philosophy of Modern Biology*, London: Collins, 1972.

Mooney, Edward F.: *Knights of Faith and Resignation. Reading Kierkegaard's Fear and Trembling*, New York: State University of New York Press, 1991.

Munk, Kaj: *Ordet*, Arnold Busck, Copenhagen: Nyt Nordisk forlag, 1963.

Nietzsche, Friedrich: *The Gay Science*, New York: Vintage Books, 1974.

Pais, Abraham: *Niels Bohr's Times*, Oxford: Clarendon Press, 1991.

Paley, William: *Natural Theology*, 1802 in William Paley: *The Works of William Paley*, Philadelphia: J.J. Woodward, no year of publication.

Peacocke, Arthur: *Theology for a Scientific Age*, Minneapolis: Fortress Press, 1993.

Phillips, D.Z.: *The Concept of Prayer*, London: Routledge & Kegan Paul, 1965.

————: *Death and Immortality*, London: Macmillan, St. Martin's Press, 1970.

Polkinghorne, John: *Beyond Science*, Cambridge: Cambridge University Press, 1996.

————: *Belief in God in an Age of Science*, New Haven: Yale University Press, 1998.

————: *Quarks, Chaos, and Christianity*, New York: Crossroad Publishing Company, 1994, 1998.

————: *Science and Creation*, London: S.P.C.K. Press, 1988.

————: *Scientists as Theologians*, London: S.P.C.K. Press, 1996.

Post, Hans: *One Man in His Time*. Oxford (Sydney): Otford Press, 2002.

Ross, George MacDonald: *Leibniz*, Oxford: Oxford University Press, 1984.

Ruse, Michael: *Taking Darwin Seriously*, Oxford: Basil Blackwell, 1987.

————: *The Darwinian Paradigm*, London: Routledge, 1993.

Sackville-West, Victoria: *Saint Joan of Arc*, London: Cardinal, Sphere Books, 1990.

Scruton, Roger: *Modern Philosophy*, London: Sinclair-Stevenson, 1994.

Sheppard, Lancelot: *The Curé d'Ars. Portrait of a Parish Priest*, London: Burns Oates, 1958.

Singer, Peter: *Hegel*, Oxford: Oxford University Press, 1983.

Smith, Huston: *Forgotten Truth. The Common Vision of the World's Religions*, San Francisco: HarperSanFrancisco, 1992.

Spong, John: *Why Christianity Must Change or Die*, San Francisco: HarperSanFrancisco, 1999.

Stannard, Russell: *Doing Away with God?* New York: HarperCollins/ Marshall Pickering, 1993.

Starbuck, Edwin: *The Psychology of Religion, an Empirical Study of the Growth of Religious Consciousness*, London: Walter Scott Publishing Co., 1899.

Stevens, Anthony: *Jung*, Oxford: Oxford University Press, 1994.

Stewart, R. J. : *The Elements of Creation*, Longmead, Shaftesbury: Element Books, 1989.

Storr, Anthony: *Freud*, Oxford: Oxford University Press, 1989.

Swinburne, Richard: *The Concept of Miracle*, London: Macmillan, 1970.

Teilhard de Chardin, Pierre: *The Phenomenon of Man*, New York: Harper & Row, 1965.

Tillich, Paul: *The Courage to Be*, London: Collins/Fontana, 1962.

Tipler, Frank J.: *The Physics of Immortality*, New York: Anchor Books Doubleday, 1994.

Toynbee, Arnold and others: *Man's Concern with Death*, London: Hodder and Stoughton, 1968.

Trouncer, Margaret: *Miser of Souls, The Life of Saint Jean-Marie-Baptiste Vianney, Curé of Ars 1786-1859*, London: Hutchinson & Co, 1959.

Underhill, Evelyn: *Practical Mysticism*, London: J.M. Dent & Sons, 1914, 1948.

Walsh, William Thomas: *Our Lady of Fatima*, New York: Doubleday & Co., Image Books, 1954.

Watkin, Julia: *Kierkegaard*, London: Geoffrey Chapman, Cassell, 1997.

Watson, Lyall: *Supernature A Natural History of the Supernatural*, London: Hodder and Stoughton, Sceptre, 1973, 1974.

Weil, Simone: *Gravity and Grace*, London: Routledge and Kegan Paul, 1963.

————: *Waiting on God*, London: Fontana Books, 1959.

White, Michael & John Cribbin: *Darwin A Life in Science*, London: Simon & Schuster, 1995.

Wilkinson, David: *God, The Big Bang and Stephen Hawking*, Tunbridge Wells, GB: Monarch Publications, 1993.

Williams, T.C.: *The Idea of the Miraculous*, London: Macmillan, 1990.

Young, David: *The Discovery of Evolution*, Cambridge: Cambridge University Press, 1992.

Zimdars-Swartz, Sandra L.: *Encountering Mary. From La Salette to Medjugorje*. Princeton: Princeton University Press, 1991.

Articles and Essays:

Anscombe, G.E.M.: "A Reply to Mr. C.S. Lewis's Argument that 'Naturalism is Self- Refuting'" in *The Socratic Digest*, No. 4, 1948.

Bryld, Christian: "Reinkarnation ligger uden for Jesu univers" [Reincarnation is outside the Universe of Jesus], *Kristeligt Dagblad* 25.6.1999.

Bultmann, Rudolf: "New Testament and Mythology" in Hans Werner Bartsch, ed.: *Kerygma and Myth*, New York: Harper Torchbooks, 1961.

Crain, Steven D. Crain: "Divine Action in a World of Chaos: An Evaluation of John Polkinghorne's Model of Special Divine Action" in *Faith and Philosophy*, Vol. 14, No. 1, January, 1997.

Dover, Gabriel A: Letter to *The Times Higher Education Supplement*, in Letters to the Editor, 5.2.1993.

Evans, C. Stephen: "Kierkegaard on Religious Authority: The Problem of the Criterion," in *Faith and Philosophy*, Vol. 17, No. 1, January, 2000.

Examiner, The: Article on new discovery about galaxies, 9.1.2004.

Goodwin, Colin: "Hawking versus Aquinas" in *Tirra Lirra*, vol. 7, No. 1, Spring 1996.

Grey, William: "Hume, Miracles and the Paranormal" in *Cogito*, Summer 1993, Vol. 7, No. 2.

Hawking, Stephen: "Is the End in Sight for Theoretical Physics?" in *Black Holes and Baby Universes*, New York: Bantam Press, 1993.

Hoare, Rupert: "Alister Kee: The Way of Transcendence", *Theology*, Vol. LXXV, No. 621, March, 1972.

Holmgaard, Jens Kristian: "Afgrundsdyb misforståelse " [Abyssmal Misunderstanding], *Kristeligt Dagblad*, 29.6.1999.

Hume, David: "Of Miracles" in *Enquiries Concerning the Human Understanding*, ed. L.A. Selby-Bigge, Oxford: Clarendon Press, 2nd ed. 1972.

Huxley, Julian: "Teilhard de Chardin" in Julian Huxley: *Essays of a Humanist*, Harmondsworth: Penguin Books, 1964, 1969.

Kirkegaard, Karl Aage: "Reinkarnation og Jesu forkyndelse"[Reincarnation and the Teaching of Jesus], *Kristeligt Dagblad*, 16.6.1999.

Knudsen, Jens Martin: *Weekendavisen*, Kultur interview: Iben Thranholm, "Hjertets Tillid" [Confidence of the Heart], 12th – 18th December, 2003.

Kristeligt Dagblad: articles about the case of Pastor Thorkild Grosbøll: 24.7.2003; 14.8.2003; 28.8.2003; 7.10.2003.

————: "Teologisk notat dømmer kirketjeners tro ude"[Theological note excludes Verger's belief], 13.1.2004.

Leibniz, Gottfried W.: "On the Ultimate Origination of Things", in G.H.R. Parkinson, ed.: *Leibniz Philosophical Writings*, London & Melbourne: Dent, Everyman's Library, 1973.

Lessing, Gotthold: "On the Proof of the Spirit and of Power" in Gotthold Lessing: *Lessing's Theological Writings*, tr. Henry Chadwick, Stanford: Stanford University Press, 1957.

Molar, Thomas: "The Cult of Teilhard" in *Triumph*, March, 1967.

Odegard, Douglas: "Miracles and Good Evidence" in *Religious Studies*, Vol. 18, 1982.

Osborn Foundation: *Special Digest*, 1972, special edition of *Faith Digest*.

Patterson, Bryan: "Seeing the light at death" in *The Sunday Tasmanian*, 3.2.2002.

————: "Soullessly clinging to survival", *The Sunday Tasmanian*, 29.9.2002.

Platt, J.E.: "Sir Alister Hardy's proposed Science of Theology" in *Theology*, Vol. LXXVI, No. 640, October 1973.

Pojman, Louis P.: "A Critique of Ethical Relativism" in Louis P.Pojman: *Ethical Theory*, Classical and Contemporary Readings. 2nd edition, Belmont, CA, Wadsworth Publishing Company, 1995.

Smart, Ninian: "Miracles and David Hume" in Ninian Smart: *Philosophers and Religious Truth*, London: SCM Press, 1964.

Steensgaard, Pernille: "Præsten tror ikke på Gud"[Pastor doesn't believe in God] interview with Pastor Thorkild Grosbøll in *Weekendavisen*, 23.5.03.

Swinburne, Richard: Richard Swinburne: "Miracles" in *Philosophy of Religion*, Selected Readings, 2nd ed., ed. William Rowe and William J. Wainwright, New York: Harcourt Brace Jovanovich, Publishers, 1973, 1989.

————: "How the Existence of God Explains Miracles and Religious Experience", Ch. 7 in his *Is There a God?* Oxford: Oxford University Press, 1996.

Time: "Cult of Death", 4.12.1978.

Villiers, Oliver G.: *Wellesley Tudor Pole*, printed by Bells of Canterbury, 1968.

Watkin, Julia: "The Criteria of Authentic Ethical-Religious Authority: Kierkegaard and Adolph Adler" in *ACME Annali della Facoltà di Lettere e Filosofia del'Università degli Studi di Milano*, Vol. XLV, Fasc. I, Gennaio-Aprile 1992.

Williams, Bernard: Williams: "Has 'God' a Meaning", in *Question*, 1, February, 1968.

Young, Robert M.: "The Impact of Darwin on Conventional Thought" in Anthony Symondson, ed.: *The Victorian Crisis of Faith*, London: S.P.C.K., 1970.

TV Programmes:

ABC TV (Australia) Compass, *Sea of Faith*, 23.3.2003.

ABC (Australia) Science online, 20.7.2000: *Hunt for gravity points to parallel universes.*

ABC TV(Australia) Compass, 1.9.2002: *Parallel Universes.*

ABC (Australia) TV, 21.1.2004: *Parallel Universes*, [BBC Two/TLC production 2002].

Australian Channel 6 TV, *Today*, 7.6.04: Interview with Raelian Tora Blackman.

BBC Two, 14.2.2002: *Parallel Universes.*

SBS TV (Australia) *As It Happened*: "Hitler's Religion", 15.8.1996.

Index

A

ABC Australia TV, 123
Abraham and Isaac, 44
Adams, Phillip, 115
Adler, Adolph, 44, 123
Agassiz, Louis, 83
Agnostic, 63, 84-85, 92, 111,
  agnosticism, 85
Altizer, J.J., 113
Altruism, 46, 95, 100, 111-112,
  altruistic, 46, 94-95
Anabaptist, 44
Anglican, young, 51
Anscombe, Elizabeth, 110, 121
Anselm of Canterbury, 28
Anthropic principle, 22, 114
Apparition, 50, see also Vision
Appleyard, Bryan, 113
Aquinas, Thomas, 113
Archangels, 48
Arithmetic, 38, mathematics, 38,
  62-63
Armstrong, Karen, 113
Arnold, Matthew, 104, 107, 113
Atheism, 25, 85, 111, atheist, 26,
  49, 84
Atkins, Peter, 9, 21-22, 42, 63,
  108, 113
Attwater, Donald, 113
Augustine of Hippo, 82
Australian family, 69

Avila, Teresa of, 52

B

Babbage, Charles, 83
Balle, Nikolai, 41, 113
Ballou, Robert, 113
Barbour, Ian, 113-114
Barrow, John, 114
BBC Two, 108, 123
Being, 8, 13-15, 19-20, 22, 25-
  30, 36-37, 39, 41-42, 44, 49,
  53, 59, 63, 65, 68-69, 74,
  76-77, 91, 94, 98, 100, 103-
  104, 107
Berger, Peter, 102, 114
Berkeley, George, 109, 114
Bernadette, 48, 50, 118
Bible, 9, 25, 40, 45, 79-82, 84,
  92, 107, 111, 113-114, bibli-
  cal, 81-82
Big Bang, 17, 23, 108, 121
Bjerg, Svend, 12, 114
Blackman, Tora, 25, 123
Blake, William, 46
Body, 24, 26, 39-41, 73, 109
Bohr, Niels, 9, 104, 119
Boslough, John, 114
Brooke, John Hedley, 85, 114
Bryld, Christian, 121
Buddhism, 109

Bultmann, Rudolf, 69, 121

C

Capra, Fritjof, 25, 114
Caricature, 103
Carter, Humphrey, 114
Catastrophe, 64, 90, catastrophes, 62, catastrophic, 68, 85
Chalice Well, 19
Chalmers, David, 114
Chambers, Robert, 111
Chardin, Pierre Teilhard de, 96, 120
Charlesworth, Max, 33, 114
Christ, 31, 33, 41, 46, 97, 112 (see also Jesus)
Christianity, 9-10, 12-15, 19, 26, 28, 30, 40, 43-44, 46, 68, 83, 85, 94, 96, 100, 110, 112, 115, 119-120
Christmas, Father, 30, Santa Claus, 60
Chalmers, David, 114
Chambers, Robert, 111
Churchland, Paul, 114
Clark, Ronald, 85, 114
Climacus, Johannes, 29, 60
Cloud of Unknowing, The, 20, 30, 113
Communication, 5, 35, 37, 39-41, 43-45, 47, 49-51, 53, 55, 57, 59
Compass, ABC Australia TV, 123
Conception, Immaculate, 50

Consciousness, self-consciousness, 93
Coward, Harold, 114
Crain, Steven, 27, 121
Creation, 5, 9-10, 14, 25, 27, 79-84, 86, 91, 94, 104, 111, 113, 119-120, creator, 27, 83-85, 88, 91, 99, 107
Creationism, 81, creation science, 119
Cribbin, John, 120
Cross, John of the, 52
Cumulative selection, 90, 92
Cupitt, Don, 13, 114
Curé d'Ars, 48-49, 116, 118-119, Vianney, 70-72, 118, 120

D

Damnation, 85
Daniken, Erik von. 25, 115
Darkness, Universal, 65, 67-68
Darwin, Charles, 79, 84, 114-115
Darwin, Erasmus, 111, Zoonomia, 111
Darwinism, 79, 81, 96, 98, 101-102, 111, 118
Davies, Paul, 23, 71, 92-93, 101, 115
Dawkins, Richard, 9, 30, 69, 89, 91-92, 95, 115
Dawson, Christopher, 115
Day of Judgement, 20
Death, Life after, 13-14, 26, 40-41, 85, 98, 104, 110, 114

Death of God, 11, 20-21, 113
Deism, 25, 84, deistic, 50, 88
Dennett, Daniel, 115
Denton, Michael, 115
Descartes, René, 24, 115
Design, 22-23, 55, 84, 88, 98, 100-101, designer, 22-23, 55, 71
Desmond, Adrian, 115
Development, 36, 86, 89, 94, 99, 110, 117
Divine, 5, 10, 12, 14, 17, 21, 23-24, 27, 31, 33, 35-37, 39-41, 43-60, 62, 64, 66, 68-69, 72-74, 77, 79, 81, 83, 85, 88, 92, 95-99, 101-104, 107, 109, 111, 116, 121, divinity, 5, 43, 46, 50, 54
Divine intervention, 10, 69, 73-74, 109
Dover, Gabriel A., 121
Drummond, Henry, 94, 115
Dual-aspect monism, 26-27, 41, 73, 93
Dualism, 24, 26-27, 36, 40, 42, 72, dualistic, 26, 40, 46, 111

E

Elizabeth I, 65
Energy, 24-26, 39, 107
Eternal damnation, 85, damnation, 85
Eternal life, 11-15, 17, 23-24, 28, 42, 94, 116
Eternal power, 54, 104

Eternity, 13, 27, 41-42
Ethics, 94, 100-101, 117
Evans, C. Stephen, 109, 115, 121
Evil, 45, 47, 80, 117, evils, 47
Evolution, 6, 74, 79, 81-101, 111, 115-117, 121
Examiner, The, 121
Existence, 9-10, 13-14, 16, 21, 24, 28-30, 35, 37, 43, 47, 53-54, 57, 79, 84, 86-87, 92-93, 98-99, 101-102, 104, 107-108, 111, 123, existential, 37, 54-55, 58
Experience, religious, 35-37, 51, 68, 74, 109, 116-117, 123

F

Feuerbach, Ludwig, 112, 115
Fogelin, Robert, 116
Freud, Sigmund, 42
Fuller, Reginald, 70, 109, 116
Fundamentalism, 14, 18-19, fundamentalist, 18-19

G

Gandhi, Mahatma, 116
Gene, 95, 115
Genetic, 89-91, genetics, 89-90, 99-100
Genesis, 5, 79-87, 91, 101, 104, 118
Genius, 46

Ghéon, Henri, 116
Gish, Duane, 116
God as fact, 36
God as value, 36, 54-57
Godhead, 20, 104, 109
Goodwin, Colin, 108, 121
Gosse, Edmund, 52, 79, 116
Gosse, Phillip, 83
Goulder, Michael, 24, 37, 51-52, 116
Grey, William, 121
Ground of Being, 14-15, 29-30
Grosbøll, Thorkild, 11-23, 105, 107

H

Haeckel, Ernst, 25, 98, 116
Hallucination, 96, hallucinations, 33, 77
Hamilton, William, 113
Hardy, Alister, 35, 68, 116, 122
Hawking, Stephen, 16, 22, 38, 114, 116, 121
Hay, David, 35, 68, 116
Heaven, 9, 13-14, 17, 20, 26, 30, 40-41, 60, 104, 107, 110
Hegel, Georg, 24, 26, 45, 112, 119
Hell, 17, 40-41
Heywood, Rosalind, 37, 77, 109, 116
Hick, John, 42, 73-74, 77, 109, 116-117
Hindu, 25, 33
Hinduism, 112

Hitler, Adolf, 104
Hoare, Rupert, 121
Holmgaard, Jens Kristian, 121
Houston, J., 117
Humanists, 59
Hume, David, 61-62, 122
Huxley, Aldous, 44, 117
Huxley, Julian, 122
Huxley, Thomas Henry, 84, 111
Høgsbro, Bente, 12, 20

I

Ideality, 49, 96, 101
Images, 30, 50
Immaculate Conception, 50
Immanence, 46, 107, immanent, 17, 26-27, 50, 54, 107
Immortal, 40-42, immortality, 40-42, 119-120
Induction, 64, 66, 102, inductive, 67
Inspiration, 81, 111
Interaction, 27, 58, 72
Islam, 81

J

James, William, 109, 117
Jeans, James, 93, 117
Jesus, 20, 28, 31-33, 40-41, 43-45, 48, 58, 61, 70, 72, 97, 103-104, 107, 121-122
Joan of Arc, 48, 119
Jonathan, 75-77

Jones, Jim, 104
Judaic, 81
Judaism, 110
Jung, Carl, 42

K

Kant, Immanuel 53
Kee, Alister, 28, 117, 121
Keightley, Alan, 36, 117
Kelvin, Lord, 15-16
Kent, John, 50, 117
Kierkegaard, Søren, 7, 29, 31-32, 37, 43-47, 59-60, 96, 104, 110-112, 117-118, 120-121, 123
Kirkegaard, Karl Aage, 42, 122
Knudsen, Jens Martin, 9, 122
Kristeligt Dagblad, 42, 121-122
Kuhn, Thomas, 16, 118

L

Lassagne, Catharine, 49
Laurentin, René, 118
Laws of Nature, 5, 61-69, 71-72, 75-77, 85-86, 88, 111
Laws of Physics, 61-63, 70-72, 77, 92-93, 108
Leibniz, Gottfried, 21, 122
Leslie, John, 108, 118
Lessing, Gotthold E., 122
Lewis, C.S., 32, 39, 51, 59, 62-63, 67, 118, 121
Lizard, analogy, 68-69
Lyell, Charles, 85

M

Macquarrie, John, 29, 118
Malcolm, Norman, 53
Malthus, Thomas, 85
Marx, Karl, 83
Mary, Virgin, 48
Material, 11, 13, 20, 24, 31, 36, 39, 42, 45, 47, 70, 81, 109, 111, materialistic, 24-25, 31, 36, 39, 98
Mathematics, 38, 62-63
Matter, 9, 24-26, 30-31, 39, 56, 65, 73-75, 94, 99-100, 108, 114
Memes, 95
Metaphysical barrier, 33, 36-37, 47, 53-55, 57, 63, 67, 71, 75, 92, 103, 108
Metaphysics, 21, 24, 36, 109
Mind, 14, 23-24, 26-27, 30-31, 37-39, 41-43, 49, 66, 68-70, 73, 83, 85, 89, 91, 93-94, 96, 103-104, 109, 111, 114-115
Miracles, 5, 17-18, 55-57, 61-75, 77, 83-84, 109-110, 116-118, 121-123
Milton, Richard, 8, 90-92, 118
Mivart, St. George Jackson, 87, 118
Modern, 1, 3, 5-6, 9-10, 12, 14-20, 22, 24, 26, 28, 30, 32, 36, 38, 40, 42, 44, 46, 48, 50, 52, 54, 56, 58, 60-62, 64-66, 68-70, 72, 74, 76, 79-80, 82, 84, 86, 88-92, 94, 96, 98, 100, 102-105, 108, 110, 112-120,

122, 126, 128, postmodern, 15, 105

Molar, Thomas, 122
Molyneux, Georgina, 118
Monism, 26-27, 41, 73, 93, monistic, 27
Monod, Jacques, 93, 118
Mooney, Edward, 118
Moore, James, 115
Morality, 95, 100-101, morals, 100
Multiverse, 93, 108, super universe, 22, 108
Munk, Kaj, 61, 75, 118
Mutation, 86, 90
Mutations, 89, 92

N

Natural selection, 83, 86-92, 98-100
Nazi, 48, nazism, 49, 104
Newtonian physics, 101
Nietzsche, Friedrich, 119
Neo-Darwinism, 79, 90-92, 101

O

Occam's razor, 76
Odegard, Douglas, 65, 122
Omniscient, 47
Omnipotent, 47
Origen, 82
Osborn, Tom L, 31
Osborn Foundation, 31, 122

P

Pact of Plenty, 31
Pais, Abraham, 119
Paley, William, 84, 119
Panexperientialism, 109
Pantheism, 24, 97, pantheistic, 25
Parallel Universes, 108, 123
Parapsychological, 36-38, 70-71, 75, 77, 94, parapsychology, 28, 36, 71, 73, 77, 109
Paris, Abbé, 65
Parkinson, G.H.R., 122
Patterson, Bryan, 122
Paul of Tarsus, 9
Peacocke, Arthur, 27, 119
Phillips, D.Z., 42, 53-59
Platt, J.E., 36, 122
Pojman, Louis, 32, 122
Polkinghorne, John, 9, 22, 26, 41, 58, 72, 84, 93, 119, 121
Polytheism, 26
Post, Hans, 48, 119
Power of Being, 29, 104
Prayer, 5, 31, 35, 47, 50-60, 74-75, 103, 119
Process, 14, 26-28, 60, 73, 84, 86, 88-90, 93-98, 101
Progress, 15, 94-95, 97-99, 102, 115
Psyche, 39-40
Psychology, 42, 120
Purgatory, 20, 110

R

Rael, Raelians, 25
Ranke, Leopold von, 102
Reductive, 57, 96
Regis, Francis, 71
Religious Experience, 35-37, 51, 68, 74, 109, 116-117, 123
Resurrection, 11, 40-42, 75, 110
Revelation, 43-46, 83, 94, revelations, 43-44
Ross, George MacDonald, 119
Ruse, Michael, 99, 111, 119

S

Sackville-West, Victoria, 119
Santa Claus, 60, Christmas, Father, 30
SBS Australia TV, 123
Science online, ABC Australia, 123
Scruton, Roger, 119
Sea of Faith, 11, 13-15, 17-19, 107, 123
Self, The, 5, 35, 38-41, 43, 56, 98, 101, 109
Shadowlands, 59
Shawshank Redemption, The, 32, 79
Sheol, 40
Sheppard, Lancelot, 119
Singer, Peter, 26, 119
Skorzeny, Otto, 49
Smart, Ninian, 122

Smith, Huston, 104, 109, 120
Social Darwinism, 98, 111
Soul, 39-42, 87, 109
Spirit, 20, 24-25, 31, 39-40, 43, 56, 94, 102, 122
Spong, John, 43, 51-52, 58, 81, 120
Stannard, Russell, 9, 82-83, 120
Starbuck, Edwin, 109, 120
Steffensen, Palle, 12, 114
Steensgaard, Pernille, 123
Stevens, Anthony, 120
Stewart, R.J., 120
Storr, Anthony, 120
Struggle for Existence, 86-87, 98-99
Supernatural, 10, 12-14, 28, 53, 62-63, 65, 69, 114, 120, supernature, 5, 11, 13, 15, 17, 19, 21, 23-25, 27-29, 31, 33, 72, 102-103, 120
Super universe, 22, 108, multiverse, 93, 108
Survival of the Fittest, 86-87, 94
Swedenborg, Emanuel, 46
Swinburne, Richard, 69, 120, 123
Symbols, 50
Symondson, Anthony, 123
Synthetic Darwinism, 89, Neo-Darwinism, 79, 90-92, 101

T

Taylor, John, 16

Teilhard de Chardin, Pierre, 96, 120

Teleology, 95, 99-101

Theism, 9, 14-15, 17, 22, 25, 28, 60, 83

Thranholm, Iben, 122

Tillich, Paul, 14, 29, 104, 109, 120

Time, 9, 11, 14-15, 17, 20-21, 37, 41, 43, 45-46, 49, 51, 55, 57, 61-62, 68, 70-71, 74-77, 82-83, 85-91, 102, 104, 107-108, 110, 116, 119, 123

Tipler, Frank, 97, 114, 120

Toynbee, Arnold, 120

Transcendence, transcendent, 15

Trouncer, Margaret, 120

Truth, views of, 54-57

U

Unconscious, 39, 42-43, 89

Underhill, Evelyn, 52, 120

Universal Darkness, 65, 67-68

Universe, 9, 14-17, 20-27, 33, 36, 39, 43, 54, 61-64, 67-68, 71-73, 79, 88, 92-93, 95-98, 102, 104, 107-109, 111-112, 114, 117, 121

V

Vianney, J.-B.-E., 70-72, 118, 120

Villiers, Oliver G., 123

Virgin Mary, 48

Vision, 49-50, 88, 102, 120

W

Wallace, Alfred Russel, 85, 93

Walsh, William, 120

Watkin, Julia, 3, 6, 10, 12, 14, 16, 18, 20, 22, 24, 26, 28, 30, 32, 36, 38, 40, 42, 44, 46, 48, 50, 52, 54, 56, 58, 60, 62, 64, 66, 68, 70, 72, 74, 76, 80, 82, 84, 86, 88, 90, 92, 94, 96, 98, 100, 102, 104, 108, 110, 112, 114, 116, 118, 120, 122-123, 126, 128

Watson, Lyall, 28, 49, 120

Weil, Simone, 53, 120

White, Michael, 120

Wilkinson, David, 121

Williams, Bernard, 13, 15, 55, 123

Williams, T.C., 121

WIN Australia, 25

Y

Young, David, 121

Young, Robert, 82, 123

Z

Zimdars-Swartz, Sandra, 121

Zoonomia, 111